# A Vision Realised

# A Vision Realised

A History of the Perse
and its move from
Gonville Place to Hills Road
forty years ago

David Jones

**The Perse School**

**Cambridge**

ISBN 0 951 6563-3-3

Photoset by E & E Plumridge Ltd in Bookman and Utopia
and printed on 130 gsm Nimrod Silk

# contents

The photographs have been taken from the archives, including copyright material from Aerofilms, Cambridge Evening News, The Fitzwilliam Museum, Edward Leigh, Photo-Reportage Ltd and Ramsey and Muspratt (Cambridgeshire Collection). Other photographs were supplied by James Payne (pages 95 – 100) and the author.
A number have been included, despite their poor quality, on account of their historical interest.

## *Introduction*

This is the story of how a long-held vision reached fulfilment against many odds. Nearly a hundred years ago, Dr W.H.D. Rouse became Headmaster of the Perse. The School had then quite recently moved from its original site in Free School Lane to new premises in Gonville Place, but Rouse soon found them too cramped for the School that was growing and flourishing under his leadership. He strove against great financial difficulties to provide the large playing fields that one day would accommodate the new buildings he dreamed of. He got no further than acquiring the fields in his time as Headmaster, but he did live long enough to see Stanley Stubbs reaffirm Rouse's grand objective and begin again the mighty task of accomplishing the move to Hills Road. This was perhaps the single most important event in the history of the Perse in the 20th Century.

It is now forty years since Stubbs's success was triumphantly recognised at the official opening of the new School by H.R.H. Princess Alexandra, on 3rd July 1961 – forty years to the day as these words are written. This publication tells the story of that move in more detail than was possible twenty-five years ago in John Mitchell's History of the Perse, and brings together many previously unpublished photographs held in our archives. Additionally, it includes Persean recollections of each decade since the 1950s and a short synopsis of the earlier history of the School from 1615 to 1890, since Mitchell's History is long out of print and its salient features not necessarily familiar to the present generation of Perseans.

The original intention was for a Millennium special issue of *The Pelican* to provide a largely pictorial history illustrating the move to the present site and the subsequent changes and additions to the buildings. However, the project grew and took its final shape thanks to a suggestion from our printer, Tim Plumridge, that the early history of the School should be included, and also the Headmaster's idea of adding a chapter of personal recollections from pupils since the 1950s. Illustrations still loom large, however: nearly 200 have been selected from a vastly greater number. During this lengthy operation, incidentally, it became apparent that several periods are under-represented in the archives, particularly the 1930s, late 1960s, 1970s and 1980s. If any reader can supply prints or negatives for us to copy and return, we would be very glad to receive them.

My thanks are due to the Headmaster, Nigel Richardson, whose idea this publication was, and to the Governors for financing it. I thank those Old Persean contributors – Victor Walne, Andrew Reicher, David Utting,

Andrew Sumnall, Matthew Jordan and James Watson – for their memories of their respective decades, James Payne for his architechtural essay and photographs and also those who provided both written and verbal information, reminiscence or correction: Chairman of the Governors, Alex Cook, former Headmasters Tony Melville and Martin Stephen, Old Perseans Cyril Alliston, E.J.N. Brookes, Frank Stubbings, David Gant and Tim Plumridge, and former members of staff Keith Barry, Tony Billinghurst, Malcolm McFarlane, David Webber and the late Michael Seymour. The notes and records of the latter, and his inability to throw anything away, provided the very stuff of history.

Staff at the University Library and the Whipple Museum of the History of Science have been of courteous assistance. Mrs Di Palmer, of the University of Cambridge Local Examinations Syndicate, was instrumental in providing me an entrée to the old Gonville Place buildings, where the Premises and Services Manager, Reg Horrod, gave generously of his time and was enormously helpful in showing me around. Two pupils, Samuel Linehan and James Watson, lent a hand in the early stages of research into the Perse material in the Cambridgeshire Collection, where Chris Jakes, as ever, could not have been more helpful.

I am also grateful to the following copyright holders for permission to use material: the Master and Fellows of Magdalene College, Cambridge (the Diaries of A.C. Benson), the Fitzwilliam Museum, the Cambridgeshire Collection, Photo Reportage, Aerofilms, *The Times* and the *Cambridge Evening News*.

Finally, I should like to thank the School's Development Director Tim Boyden for reminding me of the deadlines a busy teacher is apt to forget, and his secretary Annette Bell for her swift and accurate typing of my manuscript. Their interest in the unfolding of this story was especially encouraging.

David Jones   3rd July 2001

*Wall effigy of Stephen Perse in the Chapel of Gonville and Caius College.*

*Chapter 1*

# FREE SCHOOL LANE
# 1615-1890

The Perse is not an old school. When it was founded, nearly 400 years ago, King's Rochester and King's Canterbury had already existed for almost a thousand years. Over 300 grammar schools dated from the Middle Ages and a further 185 were created by public-spirited Tudors. By 1577, most towns had grammar schools – even places with half the population of Cambridge, such as Ely and Bury St Edmunds. For a town that was home to one of only two universities in the kingdom, the absence of an endowed free school was notable. A few short-lived private schools and the choir schools of King's and Trinity, both small and exclusively for choristers, were all that Cambridge possessed. An attempt to remedy the matter in 1576 had languished for want of funds. The situation required a benefactor of substantial wealth.

STEPHEN PERSE

Stephen Perse was born in Norwich in or about 1548. He was educated there and at Gonville and Caius College, becoming a Fellow in 1571. Ten years later he became a Doctor of Medicine, abandoned most of his academic work and set up a successful practice as a physician. When he died in 1615, he left a huge fortune of £10,000. As this was a hundred times the annual stipend of a Senior Fellow of Magdalene (a poor college admittedly), he had clearly made money in other ways, namely shrewd property investments and money-lending.

Perse had grown up in an age of exceptional charitable achievements. His will, signed three days before his death but drafted long before, was very much of the Tudor tradition in its range of benefactions. It included improvements to the roads (Maid's Causeway) and water supply (Hobson's Conduit) of the town. It provided six almshouses for poor aged widows (anyone over forty). But a "Grammar Free School" was clearly uppermost in his mind, for it appears as the first item in his will.

*Sculpture of Stephen Perse in the School Hall.*

THE FREE SCHOOL

Perse's school was large for its time – 100 local boys from Cambridge, Barnwell, Chesterton and Trumpington. Charterhouse (founded 1611)

*The Free School, Cambridge*
*by C. Wild (1781-1835)*
*This view from the north-west is the earliest exterior view of the school that we have. It shows the buildings after 1817 when they housed the newly-established Fitzwilliam Museum. The north end of the Hall is on the extreme left. The two houses (Master's and Usher's) run at right-angles to the lane. The low building to the far right contained the "master's offices" added in 1817.*

began with 40 boys, Oundle (1566) with 48. The Master's salary was also large. £40 per annum was twice the average salary for a good school and comparable with the unprecedentedly high sum of £50 per annum paid at Blundell's School (1604), which had 150 pupils. The £20 per annum paid to the assistant or Usher was correspondingly generous.

Provision was made for Perse scholarships and fellowships at his college, Caius, giving preference to scholars of the Free School. By this means he hoped to reduce the Town-Gown friction that had long been an unpleasant feature of Cambridge life. Thus the school was to be a Town school, yet with a direct connection with the University.

### THE BUILDINGS

Perse had already bought a site for the school in what was then called Lorteburn or Lithburn Lane (it does not appear as Free School Lane until 1750). The buildings cost £500 and began to go up in February 1617. The School Hall was flanked by two

*View from the south-west*

houses – one for the Master, one for the Usher – to create a three-sided court. A curtain-wall with an entrance gate to the lane closed the fourth side. This was a small-scale version of the traditional college layout.

The Hall, 64 feet long and 20 feet wide, had a hammer-beam roof and a cellar below. Access was originally via the two houses. Perse's almshouses lay to the south and the Master's garden to the north. The buildings were of brick, except for the stone corners, window mullions and gateway, above which were carved the Perse family arms. The school was ready to open in March 1618.

The buildings were typical for their time. Blundell's (1604) had a 100-foot hall for 150 boys, partitioned into Higher and Lower schools. Chigwell (1629) had a similar divided hall. Harrow (1615) had a plain schoolhouse of two storeys, with rooms for the Master and Usher above the hall – and one could give further examples. It was 1650 before the idea of separate classrooms began to feature, but not until nineteenth-century alterations did this novelty appear at the Perse.

*The Frating Estate today*

## FUNDING THE SCHOOL

It has been indicated that Perse made his fortune by money-lending and it was by a scheme of loans of his money, granted by local town corporations, that he hoped to fund his school. But the corporations were not interested in risky advances to the young businessmen whom Perse hoped to encourage. Instead, Stephen's brother and executor Martin Perse bought land whose rents would finance the School. Unfortunately, their estates, chiefly the Frating Estate five miles south east of Colchester, were never very profitable. The agricultural slump of the late nineteenth century reduced their value still further and they were finally sold in 1913. They remain farms – no real estate gold mines of the sort enjoyed by Trinity or Dulwich Colleges.

There was another regrettable feature of Perse's arrangements. In order to prevent waste and mismanagement, he specified the exact sum to be spent annually on the School but he made no allowance for inflation. The Trustees or Governors of the School – the Master and four Senior Fellows of Caius – stuck to the letter and not the spirit of the will. The once-generous salaries dwindled in real terms to a point unlikely to attract capable men.

That wasn't all. Perse calculated that when all expenses were met, there would be a small surplus of just over £6 from an annual income of £250. This, he said, should be given away by the

Trustees to whatever charities they saw fit. However, this surplus grew vastly as inflation swelled the rents while the salaries remained stationary. The charity the Trustees saw fit to receive this largesse was themselves. This virtual embezzlement continued until 1837, with predictably dire consequences for the School.

LIFE AT THE SCHOOL

Should any Persean today think he is hard done by, he should consider the rules of 1622. School began at 6.00am, with prayers at 6.30am and lessons until 11.00am . Afternoon school ran (or perhaps dragged) from 1.00pm to 5.00pm. Boys were to be "carefully and diligently taught … as well in good manners as in all other instruction and learning fit to be learned in a Grammar School." That meant almost the whole of a pupil's time was devoted to the study of Latin – hence 'Grammar school'. He would use such manuals as *Sententiae Pueriles* and *Confabulationes Pueriles* before moving on to Ovid, Virgil and Seneca. Greek was reserved for the highest forms and Hebrew was also a possibility. Pastoral care consisted of corporal punishment.

The Masters were also subject to rules. The Master had to hold a Cambridge M.A. and was not allowed to hold any other post, be it a College Fellowship or church appointment. The Usher, a Cambridge B.A. at least, had to take prayers at 6.30am but the Master could stroll in at 7.00am and could also absent himself for up to an hour a day. Neither were permitted to be "usual frequenters of taverns or alehouses and be found to be given to that evil vice of drinking", on pain of dismissal. Curiously, this ordinance makes mention of the possibility of admonishing such defaulters "after their deaths", which suggests that drinking might then have been attended with drastic consequences often enough for this clause to appear.

*Jeremy Taylor*

THE SCHOOL IN THE 17TH CENTURY

Thomas Lovering was the first Master. He was a graduate of Pembroke College and since 1615 had been Master over the choristers at King's College. He made a successful start and was soon attracting fee-paying pupils, or "non-foundationers", from as far away as Northumberland and Ireland.

In these early days appeared the first distinguished Persean, Jeremy Taylor, "the Shakespeare of divines". Taylor became a Fellow of All Souls' (a copy of his portrait there hangs in the Old Upper Library) and Bishop of Down and Connor. His highly-praised writings included a life of Christ *The Great Exemplar*, and *Holy Living and Holy Dying*, which the article in the *Dictionary of*

*National Biography* calls "a complete summary of the duties, and specimen of the devotions, of a Christian". A Royalist in the Civil War, he received from Charles I, shortly before the monarch's execution, his watch and some jewels. Taylor's posthumous influence was considerable; John Wesley was indebted to his theology.

The Perse survived the hazards of plague and Civil War, despite having a Royalist Master in a Cromwellian stronghold. He was Thomas Crabbe, the first Old Persean to hold the office (1642-1652). His sudden resignation followed (it is presumed) a quarrel with the interfering Master of Caius, William Dell, whose views on education were then considered cranky. (The Master of Caius, it will be remembered, was the Chairman of the Trustees). What happened next constituted one of the most bizarre and brutal episodes in any school's history.

GEORGE GRIFFITH AND THE CRUELTY OF CRAYFORD

On Crabbe's unexpected departure, the Usher, Robert Crayford, acted as Master for a term. He was an Old Persean and had served the School loyally since 1644, seeing his salary halved in the war years when the Frating rents could not be collected. He might reasonably have expected permanent promotion and was bitterly disappointed when instead George Griffith, a Fellow of Queens' College, was appointed Master.

His disappointment took an active form. Perhaps to make up the money he lost by not being Master (the School histories by Gray and Mitchell are not explicit about this point) Crayford introduced seven private pupils in defiance of Griffith and the Governors. Surprisingly there was no immediate reaction and Crayford became even more insubordinate, culminating in an assault upon Griffith in front of the boys: "You are a stinkinge knave: you come to steal away my due: I will take you a kick on the britch and tred in your feete."

The Governors' report just quoted tells of further violence, this time towards the boys. One Thomas Peters was "wrung by both his eares in the most violent manner that one of his eares was most cruelly torn both skinne and grissle and almost went from his head: ye said Thomas Peters going home to his mother Katherine Peters house in Cambridge with his eare so torn and bleedinge to her great affrightment, the blood running down ye body of the said Thomas Peters from his head unto his feet". John Spratford was so often whipped that his father took him away from the School. Edward Webb was hit on the jaw, then twice had his head beaten against the form. He nearly died, was five weeks before he was out of danger, and was "soe much disabled in his speech and also in his memorie, that his father to his great greife was necessitated to divert him from ye way of a scholler to a servilar employment."

Such performances would today land the perpetrator in jail. Yet although Crayford was sacked he continued to defy the Governors, refused to vacate the Usher's house and even found enough sympathisers in the town to acquire a writ asserting that he had "behaved and governed himselfe welle, quietly, soberly and honestly ", and should be reinstated. This forced the Governors into an expensive lawsuit, which took two years to come before the Lord Chief Justice. He simply passed it on to the justices of Assize, one of whom was the University Chancellor. The prospect of further expense led the Governors and Crayford to compromise. Crayford kept his house for a further year, then left to become Rector of East Grinstead. As far as we know, his parishioners kept their ears.

Griffith eventually lived down the adverse publicity. Despite further difficulties, he ruled the Perse well for thirty-four years. Many Perseans went on to the University and fifteen of them became College Fellows. Christopher Greene became Regius Professor of Physic. Sir Robert Tabor discovered the effective use of quinine to treat fever, by means of which he saved the life of King Charles II in 1678. The knighthood was his reward. When Griffith died in 1687 he left a generous bequest to the School. For this, and his selfless work as Master, he is rightly remembered in the Founder's Prayer.

THE 18TH CENTURY AND NEAR-EXTINCTION

The century 1687-1787 was, as for many grammar schools, one of decline and fall – just as sackings, feuds and court cases marked schools other than the Perse during the 17th century.

Edward Sparkes, who followed Griffith, was indolent to the point of inertia for forty years. For eighteen of those years his son, an uninspiring replica of the Master, was Usher. The establishment of charity schools in 1703 and the rivalry from King's College School saw the Perse plunge towards oblivion. By 1731 it had but ten pupils, who were taught in the Master's house. The other rooms were let to an organ builder who used the Hall as his workshop. After his death, the premises continued to be let to the highest bidder. The posts of Master and Usher, their salaries eroded by inflation to a pittance, became sinecures for the Junior Fellows of Caius, each taking a turn of a few years. The Master from 1766-1767, Samuel Reeve, later achieved notoriety by hanging himself in a lumber room at Caius, his body not being found for four months.

One boy of distinction emerged in this lamentable period. Robert Cory became Master of Emmanuel College in 1797, the first (but not the last) Old Persean to become Master of his college. In 1809 he also became Knightbridge Professor of Moral Philosophy. Timid and unworldly he may have been, but he was kindly and diligent, twice serving as Vice-chancellor.

The nadir was reached in 1785 when there were no pupils at all. Many schools disappeared between 1780 and 1860, and the Perse very nearly became one of the them. An anonymous letter to the *Cambridge Chronicle* in October 1787 shamed the Governors into re-opening the School, but within seven years the sinecure system had returned. One of the absentee Masters was William Wilkins, the architect of the National Gallery, University College London and, in Cambridge, additions to King's and Corpus Christi. It was during his brief tenure of the mastership, 1804 to 1806, that he worked on his first successful commission, Downing College. Meanwhile, the School continued to stagnate, attracting a mere handful of pupils.

## THE FITZWILLIAM MUSEUM AT FREE SCHOOL LANE

From 1816 to 1842 the School housed the Fitzwilliam Museum. The University had received a bequest of paintings from Viscount Fitzwilliam and £100,000 to build a museum for them. Until that could be done, temporary accommodation was needed. The eyes of the University Museums Syndicate lit upon the virtually redundant buildings of the Free School. The Perse Trustees gladly made available the Hall and north wing.

Ironically, the architect employed to make the necessary structural alterations was none other than William Wilkins, formerly nominal Master of the School. He lengthened the Hall and put skylights into the roof to compensate for the new bookcases which obscured the original windows.

The School itself continued in the south wing.  A new schoolroom and "offices for the Master" were built at the University's expense, in return for which it had the Hall and north wing rent-free for twelve years. Thereafter it paid £50 a year to Caius.

## THE 19TH CENTURY: REFORM OR DIE

In these stagnant circumstances, under an uninspiring Master, the School was condemned to a further period of obscurity. This was not unique. Many grammar schools were sinking with alacrity. Christ's College Brecon and Bristol Grammar School both closed temporarily, the latter for nearly twenty years. Whitgift had a master but no boys for thirty years. One Master at another school converted the schoolroom to a billiards room. Since there were no boys, he said, he made more money this way. These are just some examples.

A few glorified grammar schools, by taking boarders, were rising in public esteem and social status. But even they – Harrow,

*Robert Towerson Cory.*

*The first Old Persean to become a Professor and Master of a College; Master of Emmanuel, 1797-1835*

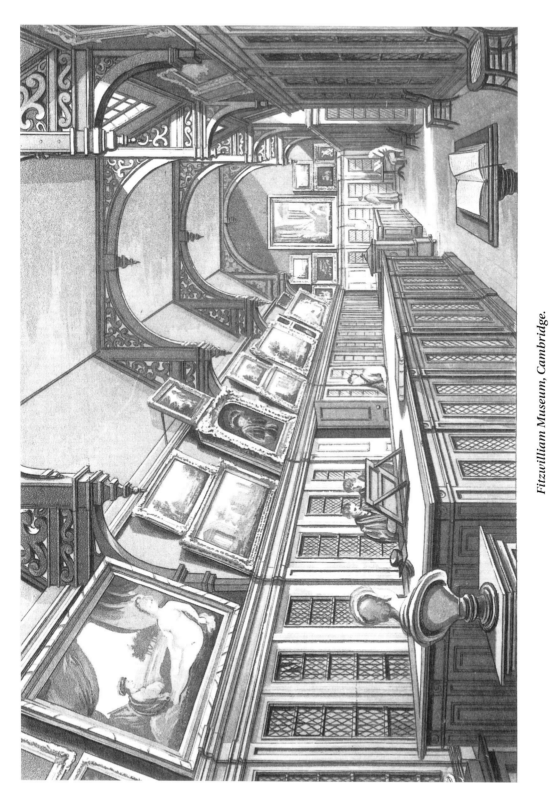

*Fitzwilliam Museum, Cambridge.*

*The earliest interior view of the Hall, after it was remodelled for the Fitzwilliam Museum by William Wilkins, 1817.*
*The view is to the north, and was drawn by R.B. Harraden.*

Rugby, Shrewsbury – had their precarious periods with numbers dangerously low. That the Perse survived, where some fifty did not, was due to two reasons common to other survivors – strong local interest in the reform and continuation of the School, and the work of one or more capable headmasters.

## JAMES BAILEY: A SUCCESSFUL EPOCH

Almost the first Master of note since George Griffith nearly 140 years before, James Bailey of Trinity College was appointed in 1825. He was a fine scholar but had struggled to find a congenial post. His merits were already sufficiently known as to recommend him to Sir Walter Scott. The great man gave him financial help on one condition only, and one still worthy of emulation. He gave 20 guineas "which I entreat you to consider as your own until better fortune shall enable you to accommodate in the same manner any young man of genius in temporary distress".

As a boy, Bailey had run away from two schools. He was determined to make the Perse the kind of school one did not run away from. He succeeded, and numbers rose from sixteen to fifty by the time he left in 1833.

Alas, his talents as a scholar were not matched by financial acumen. The post of Usher had been abolished in 1812 in order to give the Master better pay. To get any assistance, Bailey had to fund it himself. It was barely enough to keep his luckless Usher out of debtors' prison and caused Bailey financial embarrassment too. Worry took its toll and Bailey retired with a stomach ulcer, to live in relative poverty. He died in 1864.

## REFORM AT LAST: THE CHANCERY PROCEEDINGS 1837

More emphatic improvements to the moribund foundation came during a period of general agitation for reform. The Catholic Emancipation Act of 1829 was followed by the Parliamentary Reform Act of 1832 (the Great Reform Act) and the Municipal Corporations Act of 1835. Church incomes were about to be scrutinised and the Government would soon be using public funds to promote public education.

The local occasion to inquire into the Perse Trust came from within Caius College itself, for the school was not the only object of Perse's benefaction to suffer from misapplied funds. In 1830, two of the Perse Fellows complained that their stipends remained at the level set in 1615, while the Master and Senior Fellows had increased their own from the original £9 per annum to £840 per annum. This self-interested complaint led to an investigation of the whole Trust which soon entered the public arena. In 1833 a group of concerned townspeople brought the abuse of Perse's Trust to the courts.

Then all the irregularities came out. In April 1837, after a three-day hearing, the Master of the Rolls, Lord Langdale, gave judgement. It was clear, he said, that the principal object of Perse's will was the School. Any unforeseen surplus income should therefore go to the School, not into the pockets of the Trustees. A new scheme should be drawn up. However, despite evidence of malpractice, he did not remove the Master and Fellows of Caius from the Trusteeship as it was clearly Perse's intention to link the School to the College. Nor could he order the college officers to return money wrongfully appropriated on the feeble, but presumably lawful, grounds that some of the beneficiaries were now dead!

But then Lord Langdale was in a tricky position. Just a few years before, as plain Mr Bickersteth, he had been one of the four Senior Fellows in receipt of such moneys. To his credit (or was it simple prudence?) he had returned £800 and given up his Fellowship when the mismanagement first came to light. But the School saw none of the misappropriated money which, by the 1830s, amounted to nearly £1,700 per annum. The Fellows got away with it.

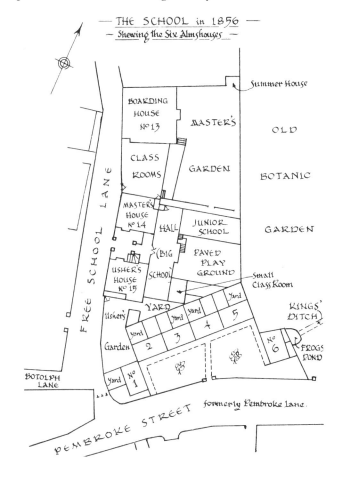

*The Hall, Free School Lane, as used for the meeting of the British Association for the Advancement of Science, 1845*

*The same view today, housing the Whipple Museum of the History of Science (looking north)*

## FREE SCHOOL LANE RENEWED

A revised scheme for the School was given approval in 1841. It restored 100 free places, gave realistic salaries to the Master and Usher, allowed for fee-paying pupils and established proper auditing of accounts. The hours, which had shrunk to five a day, were amended to seven: 7am to 5pm with breaks from 8am to 9am and 12pm to 2pm. Saturday remained a half-day. Vacations were five weeks at Christmas, five at midsummer and ten days at Easter. The two-week September absence for the Stourbridge Fair was dropped – the Fair was by then just one row of stalls, having once been one of the greatest fairs in Europe. December 14th was to be kept as Founder's Day – a commemoration the school might like to restore as we near the Quatercentenary.

The School was also rebuilt and enlarged by John Smith at a cost of £2,600. The roof of the old hall was replaced on the new hall, which had larger windows. A new Junior School was added – a smaller version of the main hall and at right angles to it – and there was a small classroom to the south. The adjacent plan and photographs best illustrate these changes. The Fellowships Board, which still hangs in the old gymnasium at the present Hills Road site, dates from this time.

Free School Lane
*c.* 1890

*The Headmaster's garden, showing the Junior School (left), the north end of the Hall (centre), classrooms (centre right) and Boarding House (extreme right). The chimney gable is of the Master's house*

*The Free School Lane playground, looking west. On the left, the small classroom, centre the east front of the Hall with the Junior School on the right*

*Free School Lane from the south-west, as remodelled 1841–2. The original gateway and wall have gone. The walls of the two houses have been raised and the roof pitch made shallower to enlarge the former attics. At ground level each house has two windows instead of one (compare page 8). The Hall is on the right.*

*The Hall looking north-west, 1890, showing the old forms, the fellowships board (extreme left), honours shields, gas jets and bell rope (to right of door)*

*The Junior School looking east, 1890. This was added to the original school in 1841*

*The Junior School looking east today. A new floor has been inserted to create upper and lower rooms*

*The Free School Lane site today from the west. Both Hall and Junior School are incorporated into the building*

MID-CENTURY INDISCIPLINE:
THE TROUBLED REIGN OF PETER MASON

The Master from 1837 to 1864 was a mathematician from St John's, Peter Mason. Once the enlarged buildings were available in 1844 numbers rose instantly to a hundred and an Assistant Usher was taken on, making a staff of three. For a time the School flourished but chiefly in Mathematics, reflecting the main competence of the teachers. Classics and English subjects were much neglected. (As was still common in schools, no other subjects were taught).

*Edward Henry Palmer*
*from the painting by*
*H.G.W. Betteridge, now*
*in the old Upper Library*

The most distinguished Persean of this period, however, was one who disliked Mathematics – Edward Henry Palmer, orientalist, linguist, journalist, barrister, foreign agent and amateur conjuror. While yet a young man he had mastered Latin, Scandinavian and Teutonic languages. He even knew Welsh and had begun to teach himself Romany while still a schoolboy, paying travelling tinkers sixpence in exchange for new vocabulary. Ill health took him from the Perse after only three years and he was twenty-three before he entered St John's College. His abilities brought him a Fellowship in 1867 and the Lord Almoner's Chair in Arabic in 1871. Ten years later, after much oriental literary work, he became a leader-writer for the *London Standard*.

Then came the events that brought him lasting fame. In 1882 Gladstone's government sent him to Egypt on a secret mission. His task was to detach the Arab tribes from the Egyptian rebels who were then threatening British interests in the Suez Canal, that vital artery of the Empire. In this he was successful.

"At the bidding of one man, many thousand wild Arabs laid down their arms, the rebellion was still-born, and the Suez Canal was saved from destruction".

But he lost his life that same year to Arab robbers: being given the choice of being shot or jumping over a precipice, he jumped. His remains were laid to rest in St Paul's Cathedral in 1883.

His biographer Walter Besant, quoted above, remarked that the Perse in Palmer's time lacked esprit de corps – no games, no societies, no "social cement". "A shy, self-conscious boy gained nothing but intellectual advantages – only part of what a school can give".

By the 1860s, matters were much worse as indiscipline grew. The Reverend T. B. Nichols, writing in *The Pelican* in December 1909, recalled a Prize-giving of Mason's time, fifty years before.

"Prize-giving day at the close of the midsummer examination was always one of tremendous importance. Then it was that the Trustees, as a body, appeared in full panoply. Then it was that we boys were supposed to be on our best behaviour, for lists were read by the Senior

Examiner, prizes were awarded, and positions fixed for the ensuing quarter. On one occasion a luckless rag-and-bone man, plying his trade in Free School Lane, had incautiously left, for a minute, his donkey-cart piled up with sacks containing all sorts of obnoxious materials. To remove one of these sacks and lodge it up against the door, which on the stroke of nine would be opened inwards to admit of the certain rush of boys, was but the work of a few moments. The consequence was, that the horrible contents of the sack were strewn all about the room, so that when the procession of Caius trustees appeared, the dons, in sheer self-defence, were obliged to have recourse to the ignominious expedient of tightly nipping their august noses, in some measure to escape from the terrible effluvium which greeted them. The disastrous consequence was that all prize-giving was suspended, no lists were read, and the boys were expelled the building."

Mason was no longer up to the job. He was often ill and absent, and grew increasingly discouraged. Separation from his wife, who had taken to drink, increased his gloom. His usher from 1861, a hot-tempered Irishman called James McDowall, was no better at keeping order. In a scene reminiscent of Crayford's attack on Griffith, the Master and Usher actually came to blows over some trivial matter, while the boys cheered them on. There had already been public protests in the local press and an intemperate slanging match between the Usher and his critics had taken place in the same journal. It was entertaining but not edifying reading and the upshot was compulsory retirement.

Mason should probably have gone long before. In his history, Sir John Gray charitably observes that Mason deserves to be remembered for the good work he did in his prime rather than for the decline occasioned by age and ill-health.

*Frederick Heppenstall*

## FREDERICK HEPPENSTALL AND THE MODERNISATION OF THE PERSE

Frederick Heppenstall became Master at a critical time (1864). Not only was the School once again in bad odour with the town but also a national investigation into the abuses of endowed schools had just begun.

The Taunton Commission of 1864 to 1868 was part of the Victorian zeal for reform, which had already embraced national and local government, public health, factory conditions, crime and poverty. The Clarendon Commission had investigated the workings of the nine best-known "public schools" in the three years preceding Lord Taunton's Commission. Now it was the turn of some 820 endowed schools of varying sizes and prestige or obscurity.

The report told an appalling tale of corruption, inefficiency and inadequacy – funds misappropriated, curricula hopelessly out of date (where teaching occurred at all), and buildings "repulsive", antediluvian, cramped and ill-ventilated. (A Sanitary Act had been passed in 1866: ventilation was much in mind). The consequent Endowed Schools Act, 1869, set up a Commission with wide powers to compel reforms, powers so extensive that it was said they "could convert a boys' school in Northumberland into a girls' school in Cornwall".

This so alarmed some schools – particularly the more enterprising and already-reforming schools – that they banded together in 1869 to form the Headmasters' Conference, which Heppenstall was invited to join in 1873. (The initiator, incidentally, was John Mitchinson of King's School Canterbury. Edward Thring of Uppingham, who is often supposed to have begun it, very nearly didn't attend the first meeting in London – but when he saw how useful it was, he suggested the annual meetings which continue to this day. In those days they met at the start of the Christmas holidays in order to avoid absence in term time).

*The Christmas Annual, 1874. The editors were Allison and Herbert Pain*

The new scheme for the Perse appeared in 1873. It ended Caius College's long control of the School and met the long-held demand for town involvement. A new governing body contained three Caius nominees and three University nominees, balanced by six Town Council nominees and three co-opted governors. Free places were reduced to twenty-five, more in response to the School's finances than to Perse's will, it would seem. Fee-paying and boarding were sanctioned, but as a town school the Perse remained chiefly a day grammar school – unlike those in essentially rural locations like Sedbergh, Sherborne, Repton and Uppingham, which changed their character and became large boarding schools.

The other notable reform was the establishment of the Perse School for Girls, which opened at 68 Trumpington Street in 1881 and moved to its present site in Panton Street two years later.

Heppenstall had already begun some of the reforms required by the Commission. He was a strong personality, rather austere, a very hard worker but prone to be over-anxious and irritable. Since he was incurably ill, perhaps this latter feature is unsurprising.

His qualities soon restored discipline and morale. He began with three assistants but ended with seven, including the first Science specialist, R.M. Lewis. His energies extended to making games an established feature of the School, even taking part in them himself, despite his poor health. (This was not as unusual as it sounds, for Masters then frequently competed with their pupils). He also introduced a house system and school colours – originally red, black and white. (It was Dr Rouse who adopted the classical purple). Lastly, a forerunner of *The Pelican* appeared in 1874: *The Christmas Annual*, written and illustrated by hand and presented to the Headmaster (his new title since the Taunton Commission) by the Sixth Form.

When Heppenstall left for Sedbergh in 1874 he had, more than anyone, rescued the Perse from its long decline and pointed the way to a new era.

## JOHN BARROW ALLEN: MORE TOWN HOSTILITY

John Barrow Allen took over a school with a growing reputation and numbers up from 119 to 175. Eight years later he was obliged to resign, having provoked a scandal that reached Parliament and *The Times.*

Flaws of character and sometimes a single misjudgement can obscure a man's merits. Allen was hard working and a good scholar, anxious to maintain high standards. But initial goodwill evaporated in the face of his autocratic methods and unnecessary outbursts of anger. That alone, of course, would not have merited questions in the House of Commons. What did was his sacking of Frederick Maxwell, a Master whom he disliked on the grounds that he was a Methodist. He alleged that other staff did not like "to work with a Master with whom they do not care to be associated out of school".

It is difficult now to comprehend this sort of religious and social bigotry, but then Nonconformism aroused strong feelings. Unluckily for Allen, leading figures in Cambridge were Nonconformists who saw his action as highly provocative. The matter was raised in Parliament, though the minister concerned declined to get involved. It was also aired vociferously in the local and national press – a Headmaster's nightmare. Allen shifted ground; belatedly arguing that he had sacked Maxwell for incompetence.

The Governors were challenged to take action against the Headmaster. M.W. Eaden Lilley, a Governor and also a Nonconformist, demanded an extraordinary Governors' meeting. After initially deciding to sack Allen, the Governors settled for censuring him, allowing Maxwell's dismissal to stand.

That was not the end of Allen's troubles, however. The Junior School or commercial side, which Maxwell had allegedly run so badly, grew even worse under his successor. A damning report in 1882 led the Governors, in the face of more Town criticism, to dismiss all the Masters working in the Junior School.

There was further uproar and commotion. Allen was accused of being interested only in educating boys on the classical side for entry to university and of neglecting the sons of (Nonconformist) tradespeople on the commercial side. The *Cambridge Chronicle*, which a century earlier had publicised the abuse of Perse's foundation, published a leading article attacking the School for once again failing to meeting Perse's intentions. They were particularly critical of the number of boarders and non-Cambridge boys receiving the benefits intended for local boys.

Allen lasted one more term before retiring. His staff and pupils gave him a decent send-off in the circumstances, but he left behind a school which, despite its notable academic record, was reduced to fewer than a hundred pupils and one regarded with marked hostility by the Town.

*Herbert Barnes-Lawrence*

HERBERT BARNES-LAWRENCE: LAST DAYS AT FREE SCHOOL LANE

Tall, urbane, gently spoken, "most courtly and tactful", Barnes-Lawrence was a commanding figure and a good disciplinarian who wielded "a long cane". Like Heppenstall before him, he was faced with a rescue job on his arrival in 1884.

Two problems stood out. Firstly, money was short. The agricultural depression had turned the Frating Estate from an asset into a liability. Repairs to the farm buildings absorbed what money there was and more besides. The School was overdrawn most years. This was particularly unfortunate in view of the second problem, the inadequacy of the Free School Lane buildings.

Since the modest rebuilding of 1841-1844, little or no improvement had occurred, at a time when many grammar schools were rebuilding on a more lavish scale and even re-locating. Ipswich School had been rebuilt on the outskirts of the town as early as 1842. Others were goaded into action by the scathing tone of the Taunton Commission in the 1860s. It found barely a quarter of the schools "fairly provided" with facilities. In Lancashire, the town schools were mostly "old, ugly, ill-ventilated [and] in every way offensive" Interiors were described as "repulsive", feebly lit through small windows. (Until the introduction of gas lighting, the Free School Lane buildings had no artificial light and school ended at 4pm in the winter). Maidstone Grammar School was surrounded by factories.

*Herbert Barnes-Lawrence,
from a photograph in
The Pelican, December 1901.
It is interesting to compare
the two photographs in the
light of the remarks at the
end of the chapter*

Portsmouth was next door to a public house. Oldham was "placed in a filthy lane inhabited by the lowest of the Irish settlers", with the added indignity of being enclosed on two sides by a slaughter-yard.

The Perse was not quite so offensively hampered. It was hemmed in, but by the University as it bought up land for its new science museums and laboratories. Beginning with the purchase of the former garden of the Augustinian Friars in 1760, used for the first Botanic Garden (which lay behind the School), the University had by 1888 acquired all the Free School Lane properties except the Perse School and almshouses. Concurrently, in 1886, the Governors decided in principle that the School should look for a new site.

This coincidence of School and University needs led to the sale of the Free School Lane site for £12,500 and the purchase of a new site from Caius, at Gonville Place, for £4,500. With additional funding from an appeal, building began in October 1889 opposite the Catholic Church, also then being constructed. The new school was ready for the Michaelmas Term 1890.

The architect was W.M. Fawcett (of whose work, more later) and the builders were Kerridge and Shaw of Sturton Street. The *Cambridge Chronicle* reported the cost to be £7,200 (excluding the purchase of the land) but Mitchell, following Gray's history, puts it at £14,500. The formal opening on 4th December 1890 was conducted by the Postmaster-General, the Right Honourable H.C. Raikes. It went on so long that by the time the toasts and speeches in reply had worked from her Majesty to the Houses of Parliament, Literature, Science and Art, the University, the Corporation and finally the School, it was nearly 5.30pm and "the audience was rapidly thinning".

The merits and defects of the buildings will be discussed in the next chapter.

Barnes-Lawrence found himself unable to remedy the School's inadequate financial endowment, something that was to dog his successor, Dr Rouse, and others since. Scholarships, bursaries and playing fields were also required, but an appeal in 1893 had limited success, coming so soon after the building appeal.

Finances apart, the work of the School continued and flourished. In 1896, forty Old Perseans were at Cambridge University, a remarkable figure for so small a school. Science had been firmly established, debating, orchestral and other societies had come into being, as had the magazine *The Pelican* (1889), while organised games took place on a rented playing field next to Fenner's (where the tennis courts are now). By 1899 numbers stood at 210 with twelve Masters.

Barnes-Lawrence left for Weymouth College in 1902 having achieved much, but believing that a younger man should now take over this still-challenging job. From fifty-two applicants the choice fell upon the thirty-nine year old W.H.D. Rouse.

*Old Persean undergraduates in 1898*

**Chapter 2**

# GONVILLE PLACE UNDER ROUSE 1902–1928

## Dr W.H.D. ROUSE

Schoolmasters rarely find their way into the Dictionary of National Biography. W.H.D. Rouse, "schoolmaster and classical scholar", earned his entry on both counts and was undoubtedly the Perse's greatest Headmaster. His scholarship earned him his Doctorate of Letters in 1903 and from that year until well into retirement he was University teacher of Sanskrit at Cambridge. He had a strong interest in folklore and was a founder editor of the Loeb Classical Library. These scholarly activities continued alongside and without detriment to his outstanding work as Headmaster.

*Dr W.H.D. Rouse*

Rouse was a short and at first sight unimpressive man. With his trim beard he looked more like a sea-captain or farmer than a headmaster. But his alert eyes and quietly authoritative speech revealed a mind and a man of distinction – even the dimmest boys recognised it. Humour and geniality were uppermost, yet combined with an unselfconscious dignity and presence. To his enemies, however, he was podgy, pushy, ill bred and cranky. Such variance of opinion is the usual reaction to strong personalities.

Rouse was strongly independent to the point of eccentricity. He hated most machines, all bureaucracy and public exams. He rode a horse or a bicycle and refused to have a telephone. Late in life, when being driven in the hated "motor car", he would sit low with his head secured under the curve of his stick or umbrella handle. He tried to run a farm from School House and had little time for Science. His love of classical authors stemmed from their continuing human appeal: their antiquity was incidental. There was nothing dead about them or their capacity, as he put it "to fill your mind with wisdom and beauty". He was a bibliophile who amassed a huge library, but he also enjoyed outdoor life and foreign travel, especially in Greece. He appreciated good food and wine. He simplified the task of buying presents by invariably giving books or wine – a commendable practice.

*Rouse's library in
School House*

## ROUSE BECOMES HEADMASTER

After brief spells at Bedford and Cheltenham, Rouse was at Rugby School when he began to look for headships. In 1900 he had been short-listed for King Edward's Birmingham, but his failure there encouraged him to look for a relatively obscure school where he could try out his educational ideas without interference. A great public school would be too circumscribed by tradition. Friends actually warned him off the Perse, pointing to its poor financial state, uneasy relations with the Town and the imminent rivalry from the first State grammar school, the Cambridgeshire High School, opening in 1902. Fortunately, Rouse ignored their advice.

## THE REPUTATION OF THE PERSE GROWS

Rouse "believed in men, not in organisation", wrote A.L. Peck, his former pupil and later Chairman of the Governors. Rouse knew it was important to get and retain good staff – then leave them alone to exercise their gifts. He soon attracted men of character and originality – Chouville, de Glehn, Appleton and others – and in 1911 one of genius, Caldwell Cook, initiator of the "Play Way". Direct Method French, German and Latin, and Caldwell Cook's Mummery for English lessons transformed teaching. Languages were learnt by "total immersion" with as little explanation in English as possible. Plays were acted, not simply read. Additionally, the aim was to make learning as active as possible and the very antithesis of cramming for exams. These ideas may seem commonplace now, but they were novel then. Moreover, it is not possible to do them justice in this brief synopsis.

Within a few years, Rouse's experiment

*Rouse's staff in 1928*

*Scenes from the Mummery: 'Baldr's Death' 1912*

brought the Perse a national, even international reputation, and a host of visitors from home and abroad. Rouse was soon thinking of expansion and rebuilding. Gonville Place was only twelve years old when he arrived but even then it had marked deficiencies.

## THE GONVILLE PLACE BUILDINGS

"The successful local boy of these years at Cambridge was Fawcett, not a man of much talent".

W.M. Fawcett, dismissively regarded here by Nikolaus Pevsner, was the architect chosen to design the new school. In the 1860s he had worked locally on church restoration and rebuilding – at Longstowe, Knapwell, Haslingfield and Elsworth. He had then been employed by Cambridge colleges. At St Catharine's he remodelled and Gothicised the (old) Hall and "made it into one of the least attractive of Cambridge College Halls". He built "a dull range" north of the Chapel at Queens', and was later to do work for Emmanuel and Hughes Hall that was (according to Pevsner) either dull or eclectically confused. The Cambridge reader can judge for himself.

Most recently Fawcett had built the Cavendish Laboratory in Free School Lane and the Local Examinations Syndicate in Mill Lane. He also had experience of building a school, the King's College Choir School in West Road, which cost £4,000 in 1877-8.

His design for the Perse did not find complete favour with the *Cambridge Chronicle* which reported the opening:

"The external appearance of the new school building cannot be said to have a very imposing or prepossessing appearance. The conveniences and accommodation of the interior, however, are everything that could

*'Rouse the Horseman'*
*by D.C. Bolton*

*Gonville Place, 1890*

*The Chemistry laboratory, 1892*

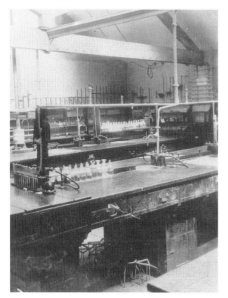

be desired. It is built in the style of the end of the 17th Century and it is constructed of red brick and tiles with ornamental work in terracotta."

The photographs and plan, with their captions, show the details of the new school. It was built to accommodate 300 boys in a Hall and twelve classrooms. The Hall was reckoned to be sufficiently impressive, though it doubled up as assembly hall, concert hall, theatre, gymnasium and classroom. Otherwise, the facilities were somewhat limited, even for the time. There were no science laboratories at a time when science teaching was clearly going to become more important. (The splitting of the atom was later accomplished a few yards away from the old Perse site in Free School Lane, in Fawcett's Cavendish Laboratory). A laboratory was tacked on rather awkwardly, following a grant from the Borough Council in 1892: the fume cupboard vented near the Headmaster's study. Rooms 1 to 3 were also later fitted out as laboratories.

There was no proper library or gymnasium, no dining hall. Staging for plays consisted of temporary blocks which barricaded the Headmaster's door to the Hall. There were no playing fields and the playground was small. Fives courts were added in 1893, providing some games facilities

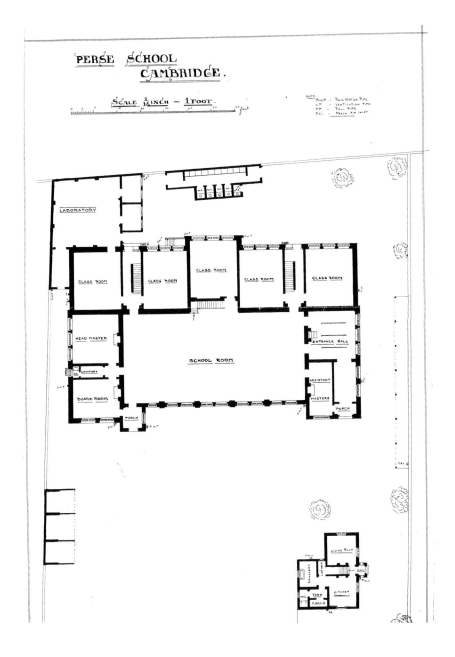

PERSE SCHOOL
CAMBRIDGE.

SCALE ½ INCH = 1 FOOT.

NOTE
R.W.P. = RAIN WATER PIPE
V.P. = VENTILATION PIPE
F.P. = FALL PIPE
F.A.I. = FRESH AIR INLET

LABORATORY

CLASS ROOM   CLASS ROOM   CLASS ROOM   CLASS ROOM   CLASS ROOM

HEAD MASTER

LAVATORY

BOARD ROOM

SCHOOL ROOM

PORCH

ENTRANCE HALL

ASSISTANT MASTERS

PORCH

LIVING ROOM

SCULLERY   YARD   KITCHEN

W.C.   COALS

*Undated plan of Gonville Place, but after 1893 as it shows the laboratory of 1892 and Fives courts (bottom left) of 1893. The classrooms were numbered 1 to 5, left to right.*
*The drawing opposite, by the architect William Fawcett, shows a clock with a niche below, intended to hold a statue of Stephen Perse, but neither of these features materialised in the finished building*

within the site. The School was at the busiest road junction in Cambridge, and the bells of the new Catholic Church were sometimes sufficient to bring lessons to a halt.

Most significantly, the site was cramped and there was limited scope for even modest expansion, let alone the grandiose schemes of Dr Rouse as the School grew rapidly successful and famous.

*View of the Perse from the Catholic Church, c. 1902 Note the absence of the clock and the statue over the right-hand door*

*Hall interior, c. 1902*

## THE SEARCH FOR PLAYING FIELDS

It was the search for playing fields that in the first instance opened the way for a new school. Hitherto, Parker's Piece had been used (shared with other clubs) and other temporary expedients had been tried with college grounds. A solution was eventually found, thanks to Trinity College.

Trinity owed the Perse a favour. In 1896 they had closed their choir school and Barnes-Lawrence had allowed the boys to transfer to the Perse. In 1905, Trinity agreed to lease a field belonging to its farm near Luard and Hills Roads. Three years later, the School was able to buy it. The purchase was partly funded by the Old Persean Society whose Secretary since 1901, H. P. Cooke, proved indefatigable in promoting the interests of the School.

The ground had to be levelled first, since the ridge of a Roman road ran through the site. (The line of it runs from Long Road, through the present Geography Room, and out by the cloister drinking fountain to exit the field by the third house left of the Luard Road gate). A section was cut through the ridge before it was destroyed in 1910: in a side ditch near the present rifle range they found a coin of the Emperor Septimius Severus (193-211 A D).

## ROUSE'S AMBITION FOR A NEW SCHOOL

Since the acquisition of the Luard Road fields in 1908, Rouse had begun to dream of a new school on that site. This would involve the purchase of adjacent fields. In 1914, the ever-active Old Persean Society, which had recently made a grant to establish the Glebe Road boarding houses in 1911, now took a new initiative. With the Tercentenary of the School due in 1915, they decided to launch an appeal for funds, to merge with the existing Old Persean Donation Fund.

*A early view of School House (on the right) and Hillel House from the south-east*

The matter came before the Governors in April 1914. The chairman, A.I. Tillyard, announced the intention to appeal for the huge sum of £100,000. There was astonishment from at least one quarter. A.C. Benson, himself a former schoolmaster (at Eton) and now a Fellow of Magdalene, and a Perse Governor since 1911, commented scornfully in his diary on the aim "to build such a school as Rouse's soul desires, a sort of clinic – he wants forty more rooms than he has now got, for 250 boys. I never heard such stuff".

There was probably an element of jealousy, not to mention social snobbery. Benson had been strongly placed to be Headmaster of Eton back in 1904 but had declined to stand, being too uncertain of his ability. Here was Rouse succeeding in revitalising education – and gaining a national reputation – in a way that Benson might have wished for himself. What he called Rouse's "cocksureness" grated on his sensibilities. Later that year he wrote of another meeting; "Rouse came in and was incredibly insolent. He suggested that if the governors could not find money from the School revenues for his schemes, they were bound to provide it out of their own pockets! I dished him by referring it to a finance committee. Rouse gave me a look of hatred".

*The plan of the Trinity Farm site, 1924 showing plots A and B, purchased in 1922*

The outbreak of war also "dished" Rouse for the time being, though the two houses flanking the School were bought, Pendeen House in 1914 and Gonville House in 1919. After the war, two ex-army huts were erected in the garden of Pendeen House – temporary expedients which remained for nearly forty years, one bearing the stencilled "Lot 14". These house purchases would increase the value of the site when eventually sold and would meanwhile ease the present cramping.

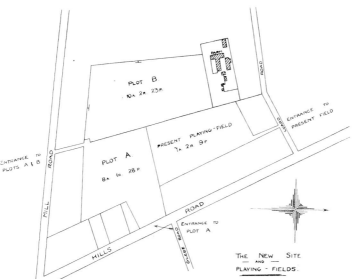

Once the war was over, however, the Governors took the decision, in principle, to build a new school on the Hills Road playing fields. Trinity College was prepared to sell a further nineteen acres of the farm fronting Hills Road (see plan), which was purchased in 1922. The money came from the Tercentenary and War Memorial Funds, plus a large donation from

Nottingham industrialist Sir Harold Bowden, after whom the subsequent cricket pitch was named. Dr Rouse's completion of twenty-one years as Headmaster (1922) was also used as an occasion for fundraising, it being his "express wish that no testimonial of a purely personal nature should be offered to him" and that the money should join the Tercentenary Fund.

Speaking at the Old Persean Dinner on 12th November 1920, H. P. Cooke said that unless the School was rebuilt, its special character and value could not be maintained. The Governors "must call a new school into existence to save and develop the virtues of the old".

But with the purchase of the field, there matters rested. Funds were insufficient to take the plan any further. Without either a substantial accumulation of capital or a "millionaire friend", as Rouse put it in 1926, a new school remained a dream. Rouse did not give up. He returned to the theme on Speech Days, and at the annual Old Persean dinners, until he retired in 1928. The School site "would make a beautiful Selfridge's store", he urged in 1926. He hoped that "before he was in his grave he might see the new school raised on the ground which he was now using to grow potatoes". Alas, he never saw the new school, but he did live long enough to meet Stanley Stubbs, Headmaster from 1945, and to know that the move was at last going to happen.

Before that, however, came the reign of Mr Wootton, who had very different ideas.

*An early view (probably pre-1914) looking south-east from School House towards Lime Kiln Hill, later obscured by the development of Mowbray Road and Queen Edith's Way*

*Chapter 3*

# GONVILLE PLACE UNDER WOOTTON 1928–1945

## H. A. WOOTTON

H. A. Wootton came as something of a shock after Dr Rouse. Rouse had been genial: Wootton was rude. Rouse was slow to anger: Wootton was a frequently erupting volcano. Rouse saw his staff as colleagues and friends: Wootton saw them as subordinates and potential enemies. Rouse binned unnecessary paperwork: Wootton produced it. Rouse hated public exams: Wootton embraced them. "What had been an exceptionally happy school soon became a very unhappy one," wrote John Mitchell, from personal experience, in his 1976 history of the School.

*H.A. Wootton*

The Governors had done what many schools have done before and since; in endeavouring to correct the perceived weaknesses of the outgoing Headmaster they had gone to the other extreme. Distinguished staff were rapidly alienated and left or retired early. Prospective parents were put off and numbers dropped, a situation not improved by the economic Depression of the early 1930s.

What were the Governors trying to correct? Firstly, the relative neglect of Science. Wootton, who had spent nine years as Headmaster of Kingswood School, Bath, had previously been Chief Science Master at Westminster School and had written two text books on Chemistry. Secondly, Wootton had obviously demonstrated administrative ability in his first Headship, whereas Rouse was known to have had scant regard for the niceties of organisation. Then, Rouse's disinclination to put boys in for public exams (School Certificate and Higher School Certificate in those days) was not always reassuring to parents who liked to see some tangible evidence of their sons' achievements. In Rouse's later years, some thought discipline had grown slack. And of course there was still the vexed question of accommodation, which Rouse had not been able to solve.

## DEVELOPMENTS UNDER WOOTTON

The individuality of the Perse probably seemed more like eccentricity to Wootton. He was more concerned to adopt "what he supposed to be the approved public school procedure", as John Mitchell put it. Wootton announced his intention to bring the curriculum "into line with the usual national pattern". Science was given its proper place. Physical Training was reformed. The long forms in the Hall were cleared out to allow the use of gymnastic equipment, and lessons were given by a qualified instructor, Mr F.G. Finch. The use of corporal punishment was now reserved for the Headmaster alone.

*The Hall during a PT lesson with 'Ferdie' Finch. The portraits of Edward Palmer and Jeremy Taylor can be seen on the back wall.*

Many of Wootton's changes were practical as much as educational. A telephone was installed and a full-time secretary appointed, soon followed by a part-time clerical assistant. Board of Education forms were returned promptly. Better lighting was introduced. Wootton was undoubtedly an efficient organiser, though he produced a stream of paper and some friction amongst staff who were not allowed to use their discretion, even in small matters. Naturally, Wootton very soon turned his mind to improving the inadequate buildings.

## THE DECISION TO STAY AT GONVILLE PLACE

Wootton made the decision to stay at Gonville Place very early on and before the economic Depression had exacerbated the School's financial difficulties. On Speech Day in December 1929 he made clear his opposition to a move. Why was this? Some of the arguments offered publicly were incredible in the light of what had been said before. The site was deemed to have ample space for expansion. The position was said to be light and airy. The classrooms, situated as they were behind the Hall and therefore furthest from the main road, were said to be protected from noise and disturbance. The most strongly urged considerations were the historical associations of the site – nearing its fiftieth anniversary – and its proximity to both the Town centre and University on the one hand, and the railway station (whence came the "county" boys) on the other. The School lay half way between the Senate House and Station Road.

There was, however, another influence of some significance. Dr Rouse had retired to nearby Histon Manor and still kept himself informed about the School. Wootton, who wanted to make his own mark and stamp his authority on the School, must have felt uneasy lest he seemed to be in the shadow of this legendary yet still very present great man. Personal animosity rapidly sprang up between the two, and John Mitchell, in his School history, believed that this was a considerable factor in Wootton's decision. It was an emphatic way of closing the Rouse chapter.

In 1930, an interim inspection by the Board of Education took place. Like their colleagues in 1922, the inspectors emphasised that the buildings were unworthy of the School. There was no proper library, no gymnasium, no art room. A cramped hut was used for "Manual Instruction" (the 'thirties equivalent of Technology). Science facilities were compared unfavourably with those at the County school. The staff room was too small and there was no dining hall. The absence of a library was seen as particularly regrettable in a school renowned for its language teaching. The inspectors argued that Gonville Place would not now be an obvious choice of site. The southward spread of Cambridge, along with improved traffic facilities, made a move to the playing field site a more sensible option. They felt that failure to move might later be regretted, but recognised that financial practicality was the determining consideration.

Nevertheless, Wootton did not alter his view that the School should stay at Gonville Place. The Governors vacillated. Until now they had been searching for a buyer of the site. In 1925 they had nearly sold Gonville House to the Ortona Motor Company (the local 'bus company) and a 'For Sale' sign remained on the premises until October 1931. The general expectation had been that Wootton would continue the work towards rebuilding at Hills Road. But Wootton's counter-arguments prevailed. On 30th October 1931 the Governors finally agreed to keep the School where it was. In February 1933 Plot A (see map) was sold back to Trinity to help finance expansion at Gonville Place.

GONVILLE PLACE EXPANSION 1933-1934

With the decision made, Wootton turned his considerable organising ability to the task of raising funds. A Building Fund was established and

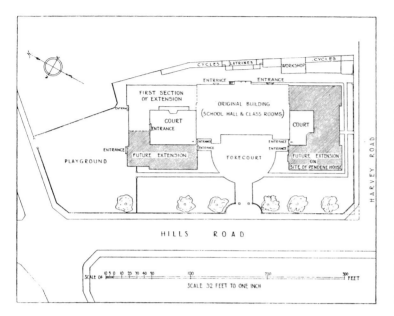

*Proposed development of the Perse at Gonville Place. Only the first phase was built*

an appeal sent out via the newly-formed Friends of the Perse School. The Parents' Committee of that body organised regular fetes and other fund-raising activities. Part of the playing field was sold, as mentioned above.

Before these funds were raised, however, the Governors boldly went ahead and borrowed most of the £12,000 needed for the first phase of the planned extensions. The covenanted donations would then – it was hoped – pay off the loan and interest year by year. This was, of course, during a serious economic recession when Masters' salaries had already been cut by ten per cent.

In February 1933 the architect, W.A. Forsyth, submitted his plans, which are reproduced here. *The Pelican* of December 1933 describes them thus: "The underlying principle of the scheme is that when all extensions have been completed the north west or Gonville House Court shall consist of Science Laboratories and a Gymnasium together with rooms for the Officer Training Corps and Scouts, while the south east or Pendeen House Court will consist of large classrooms, a Dining

*The architect's impression of the proposed extensions at Gonville Place*

Hall, and Kitchen and Art Room." Until the later extensions could be built, the Dining Hall, Kitchen and Art Room were to be housed in the first-stage extension, since these were seen as immediate requirements. When they transferred to the southeast court, the vacated spaces would become extra Science laboratories. In the event, of course, only the first stage was ever built.

The firm of Sindall began building in July 1933 and on 18th November the foundation stone was laid by the Vice-chancellor of the University,

*Vice-chancellor J.F. Cameron lays the foundation stone, 18th November 1933*

J.F. Cameron (appropriately the Master of Caius College). Under the stone was placed a casket containing a list of the Governors, Staff and members of the School. The stone does not appear to have survived the modifications made when the building was later taken over by the Local Examination Syndicate. On the same occasion the Friends of the Perse presented a portrait of E.H. Palmer, resplendent in his Arab robes. It is a copy, by H.G.W. Betteridge, O.P., of the portrait which then hung in St. John's College Hall (see pages 22 and 40).

The extension was ready by the Michaelmas Term of 1934 and was formally opened on 16th November by the Right Honourable Stanley Baldwin M.P., the Chancellor of the University and soon to become Prime Minister for the third time. Significantly, Dr Rouse was not present, a fact which Baldwin regretted

*Stanley Baldwin at the formal opening of the new buildings 16th November 1934*

in his speech. However, he praised the decision of the School to remain an integral part of Cambridge "instead of following the modern tendency to remove old historic foundations away from the town". He unlocked the new buildings almost unseen in the dark until, with dramatic effect, all the lights came on as the key turned.

*The Pelican* for December 1934 commented on the new buildings: "...the extension is a great success, for externally it blends harmoniously with its surroundings; the general style of the old part has been

*The new buildings, showing their relation to the old*

*The new chemistry laboratory*

followed and similar brickwork and roofing used.

Inside, however, one is at once struck by the spaciousness and modernity of the rooms. The windows are of modern steel-framed type and of very large area; heating is by means of the latest flat radiators, in many cases fitted high up on the walls. As a general decoration scheme, natural teak and pine, in conjunction with pale green stained pine and light buff sprayed walls have been employed".

The conveniences and advantages of the new accommodation were described, with praise for a dining hall "of considerable size", seating up to fifty (!) boys. A nice attention to detail was displayed in providing crockery with the School crest. With new heating apparatus "we now work in conditions of comfort formerly unknown". Miscellaneous sheds and the old Chemistry laboratory at the back of the School had been swept away and a new central door had been cut into the front of the Hall. One interesting suggestion by Wootton did not come to pass – the dismantling of the Free School Lane Jacobean roof and its reconstruction in the extension.

Notwithstanding these improvements, the Inspection of 1935 reported that "only the most urgent requirements" had been met. Unfortunately, despite the appeals of the Friends of the Perse, funds were not yet sufficient to begin the next stage of building. Numbers in the School had fallen too, from 356 in 1929 to 282 in 1934. In the boarding houses the picture was equally alarming: 16 boys in School House (which could hold 30) and 14 in Hillel House. The drop in numbers led the Board of Education to withdraw the Special Grant for Direct Method and experimental teaching, which had been received for many years.

THE SECOND WORLD WAR

The outbreak of war in 1939 put an end to immediate aspirations for further building, and nearly put an end to the buildings altogether. In January 1941, incendiary bombs hit the School. Only the new extension and Pendeen House escaped damage. As much havoc was caused by water as by fire. The Hall and upper classrooms were open to the sky and there was no heating or lighting – and this in the middle of a bitterly cold spell in which the fire brigade's water froze into icicles.

Amazingly, Wootton re-opened the School within days, chiefly using premises generously loaned by the Technical College (now Anglia Polytechnic University). By November, thanks to funds from the War Damage Commission and quite stupendous efforts by Wootton, the repairs were completed and the School reassembled in its own home.

*Bomb damage 1941*

## WOOTTON'S RETIREMENT

The stress of these years took a heavy toll on Wootton. He had already been briefly hospitalised in 1939 with a duodenal ulcer. In October 1940 his house in Barrow Road was wrecked by a bomb which landed in his neighbour's front garden, and in September 1941 the house he had moved to in Huntingdon Road received the close attention of another bomb. By the spring of 1944 Wootton was chronically ill and this so affected his temper and conduct that the staff actually made representations to the Governors.

In 1945 Wootton resigned. The combination of overwork, stress and his own rigid personality had broken his health and he died two years later. He had worked hard for the School but his difficult personality cast a cloud over his achievement, which was further darkened by the strains of war. Post-war reconstruction would be a big task for his successor.

## RECOLLECTIONS OF LIFE AT GONVILLE PLACE

by FRANK STUBBINGS

"My school days were passed wholly in the old buildings opposite the Roman Catholic Church, and though I was there for the additions to it in Wootton's time my actual memories of it in use seem almost confined to the basic building, before its additions. In 6th Form years (Lower VI and Upper VI) most of my lessons were in the classical VI Form room, which was against the northeast angle of the old School Hall. The Hall itself was used for daily morning assembly – in Rouse's day little more than the collects from Church of England Morning Prayer, read by the Old Man himself; there were also brief evening prayers read by him or the Second Master, Parker Smith, at the end of afternoon school on Monday, Wednesday and Friday. The Hall was also, for the last period on Saturday mornings, the venue for the whole school for community singing – items included English folk songs, ditties in French and Latin (*En passant par la Lorraine* to *Gaudeamus* and *Mihi est propositum*): I still regard those periods as a most valuable part of my education. The Hall was furnished with, I think, three blocks of long benches across its width, Fellowships [Board] at the north end of the room, rows of

*A classroom in the 1934 extension. The master (unidentified) sits on a raised platform of the kind that features in the anecdote about R.D. Hicks ( see facing page)*

individual shields on the upper walls; and a special board commemorating the great Arabist Edward Henry Palmer, on which Rouse always gave a special little discourse at assembly once a year.

Pendeen House was still used for quite a lot of teaching – we classics went there for "subsidiary" French and German and English Literature and History. French and German were mostly a matter of reading texts with native student speakers of those languages – we had the basics from Chouville and de Glehn in earlier forms of course.

How many O.Ps now can recall the mini-rifle range used by the O.T.C. in the narrow space against the north boundary wall of the old School? A few daredevils were reported to have taken pot shots at the Roman Catholic Church weathercock, not without success. When it was last taken down for repair I am very credibly informed that a bullet hole was found in the tail-feathers, attributed to G.C. Baldwin.

A feature of the old classrooms were the built-in platforms for the teachers' desks. The space below it was accessible only for storage; but one notorious naughty boy is alleged to have spent a whole lesson below it with an electric torch and a novel. At the end of the lesson the master (R.D. Hicks – reckoned a soft touch for malefactors) dictated sentences for translation to Latin in homework, including: "The master does not know the boy is under the desk". Game set and match to Hicks.

I remember the Mummery in Pendeen House from my first years (1925 *et seqq.*) – both for reading Shakespeare (Julius Caesar and Richard II particularly), also for "stick-wagging" and "Speeches". We used of course the Jacobean furniture. Marking the "speeches" was by communal vote of the class – marks for interest and marks for style, with Caldwell Cook acting as "moderator". The Tiring House was in the basement rooms below Pendeen House.

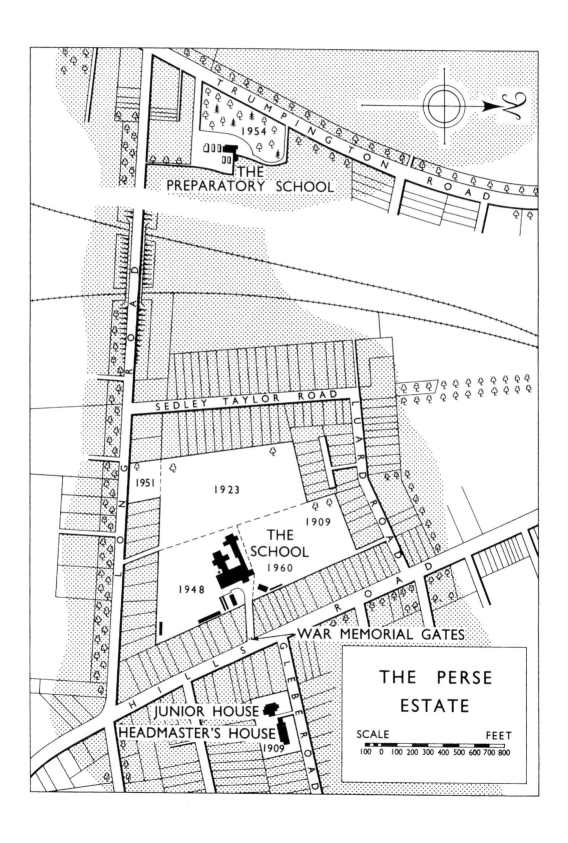

*Chapter 4*

# STUBBS AND THE MOVE TO HILLS ROAD

## STANLEY STUBBS

On Wootton's retirement there were seventy-nine applicants for the Perse Headship – an unusually large list. The School had an enviable national reputation and its academic record was impressive. There was a remarkable number of Persean undergraduates at Cambridge, while the tally of college fellowships held would have been the envy of much larger schools. On the other hand, the difficulties of Wootton's last years had lowered morale, numbers and local esteem. The new man would have a daunting task, yet one with exciting possibilities.

The fact that Stubbs had a business background may have influenced his appointment. Although the idea of moving the School was by no means yet resurrected in the minds of the Governors, the awkward state of the School's finances remained a matter of concern. Stubbs had not gone straight to university from Newcastle High School (Staffordshire) but had spent five years at Doulton Potteries, becoming manager of the large U.S.A. export department by the age of 23. He was later to say how grateful he was for his time in business.

*Stanley Stubbs*

The academic world, however, reasserted its pull and in 1930 he went up to Emmanuel College to read Modern Languages. After post-graduate teacher training he spent only five years at Gresham's School before becoming Headmaster of Soham Grammar School in 1940. His success there recommended him to the Perse Governors and in September 1945 he took up his new post as thirty-ninth Headmaster of the Perse.

Stubbs's arrival coincided with the end of the War. As the Head Boy of the School, Peter Armitstead, put it in a later tribute to Stubbs: "We were ready for a fresh start under new leadership – and this is what happened". The urbanity, assurance and courtesy of Stubbs made an immediately favourable impression, as did the "smile and crisp voice, the friendliness and the directness of the man".

The boys found Stubbs and his wife Margaret genuinely interested in their lives and concerns, while the Staff felt positive relief that the new Headmaster was approachable and at the same time trusting, allowing them to teach in the ways they thought best. In this, Stubbs resembled Rouse, and he took the trouble to inform himself of the School's past and its traditions, which he viewed with knowledge and understanding. Indeed, one of the first things he did was to visit Dr Rouse, who was still enjoying a long retirement at Histon Manor.

### "GO FORTH AND PROSPER!"

Dr Rouse, now 82, had lost none of his interest in the School he had done so much to make famous. Sixth Form Classicists still came to tea, often to read Homer, sometimes in company with "nymphs" – Rouse's habitual code-name for undergraduates from Girton. (It may be necessary to remind some readers that this was then an all-female college). A new Headmaster, however, was initially to be greeted with some reserve. But when it became apparent that Stubbs was eager to realise Rouse's dream of new premises at Hills Road, the atmosphere quickly warmed. After one early meeting, in John Mitchell's words, Rouse "stood up like an Old Testament prophet and bade Stanley 'Go forth and prosper!'"

It was a particularly happy fulfilment. Rouse was growing very old, and though he had always been remarkably hardy he was becoming less mobile and could not go on living alone in the leaky old manor. In 1948 he moved to Hayling Island in Hampshire, to be looked after by cousins, and there he died in February 1950. What would have been his last thoughts about the School had he died five years earlier? As it was, he lived long enough to see the Perse restored to happiness and esteem. By 1949, war damage was made good, numbers in the School had risen, the Perse Players, the Mummery and many societies had been revived, and a Naval section of the CCF had been established. Moreover, Rouse died in the knowledge that the School's long-awaited move might yet come to pass.

### THE EXTENSION OF THE PLAYING FIELDS, AND OTHER PRELIMINARIES

History tends to telescope time, so it is worth emphasising that a whole decade passed before the move became a practical possibility. During that time, however, Stubbs kept the move in mind and took advantage of opportunities as they arose.

In 1947 an Appeal for a war memorial fund was begun. This raised enough money to re-purchase the eight acres of Plot A (see earlier map) in 1948. Three years later, the School bought the two acres bordering Long Road, originally zoned for housing. That completed the acquisition of the Perse Estate, 28 acres in all. Only the Trinity Farm buildings and immediate yards found another developer, eventually forming Luard Close.

*The War Memorial Gates c.1954*

An important symbolic development came in 1949 with the commissioning of the fine entrance gates to the playing fields. This was also funded by the War Memorial Scheme. While playing fields might be expected to have some sort of entrance and mark of ownership, the monumental nature of these wrought-iron gates, with their brick piers and carved pelicans, was as clear an indication as there could be that one day these would lead to the new school. Designed by Robert Hurst, O.P., they were made by Raymond Lister. The pelicans are worthy of comment. In the early 20th century it was common for stone working to be done with pneumatic tools. The sculptor C.J. Whitaker carved the one-ton Ketton stone blocks entirely by hand, using hammer and chisels. He was then 82 years old. The gates were ready by 1953. There was no ceremonial opening, although it had been hoped that the Duke of Edinburgh might be present at such an event.

*Joseph Berman*

For one contributor to the war memorial, the gates had an especial significance. Joseph Berman, a Latvian Jew, had been a boarder at Hillel House (the Jewish boarding house). He was at home in Riga when the war broke out and subsequently spent the years 1941-1945 in one death camp after another. His survival was nothing short of miraculous. In a moving letter to the Treasurer of the War Memorial Fund in 1954, he wrote that in those appalling years his mind often went back to the

Perse playing fields and the kind of training in prowess and endurance that they represented. To him, the gates, lending a dignity to those fields, were an especially appropriate tribute to the war dead. It was fitting that he should later be able to revisit the School and once more experience the green spaciousness, on a perfect summer's day in 1995, just a few months before his death.

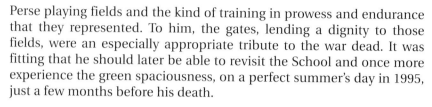

*The Macfarlane-Grieve Pavilion, 1935*

One consequence of the purchase of the extra field was that the old rifle range – a banked trench dug by the boys, lying roughly on the site of the present Masters' Common Room – now lay not at the edge of the School field but in the middle. It was therefore decided, in 1951, to build a new range. Before the old trench was levelled, archaeologists confirmed the line of the Roman road (mentioned in Chapter Two), revealing the flanking ditches and a rubbish pit containing pottery and terracotta toys and dolls of c170-200 AD. The new range by Luard Road was completed in 1954. A brick pavilion already existed, built in 1931 at the expense of Gavin Macfarlane-Grieve as a memorial to his brother Alwyn, killed in the First World War.

One further addition, which must have seemed temporary at the time but which is still with us, was the Thatched Hut – now with tarred felt replacing the thatch. (It is, of course, still called the Thatched Hut, a point of confusion for new boys). It was bought for £50 as a leftover from the Royal Show of 1951 and, in its original position next to the pavilion, served as a ladies' lavatory. It is now used as a games store.

A less useful, though picturesque, feature of the field is also still present – the small lake which appears in the southwest corner of the field after prolonged winter rain. In 1951 it flooded the garden of the Long Road house most nearly adjacent and led to some exchange of letters. Whatever alleviation resulted from the inspection of the surface drain, no lasting remedy was found, and Lake Billinghurst – a name coined in 1977 with reference to that master's exploits as an expedition leader in Spitzbergen, Iceland and Greenland – continues to put in periodic appearances.

*Lake Billinghurst, Winter 2000*

## THE PREPARATORY SCHOOL MOVES, 1953-1954

Before there were any further developments at the Upper School, the future of the Preparatory School came up for consideration. The lease of the Bateman Street site, where the School had been since 1910, was due to expire in 1963. While that was still ten years off, some thinking needed to be done soon, especially if it was thought necessary to re-locate the School, whose buildings were increasingly inadequate.

In January 1953 the Governors considered the possibility of rebuilding on the newly extended playing fields. That would have considerably reduced the field area if the Upper School also subsequently moved there, so it was fortunate that a year later a suitable alternative appeared. Leighton House in Trumpington Road, the former home of retailer Robert Sayle, and since the war in the possession of the Ministry of Works, came onto the market at £12,550. Stubbs and the Governors agreed that this was the solution. The Bateman Street site was sold to the Davies School of Language for £3,361, and a loan of £10,000 made up the sum necessary to buy Leighton House in February 1954.

*Leighton House in the 1950s*

One of those nice touches of detail occurred when it was found that Robert Sayle's initials appeared, in stone, over the porch. By chiselling out the leg of the R, PS (Perse School) was simply achieved. Little conversion work was needed, and the new school was ready to open by the Michaelmas Term 1954. Stubbs reported to the Governors: "The purchase opens a new chapter in the history of the Perse".

## 1956: THE YEAR OF DECISION

Ironically, it was the growth of the public examinations so hated by Rouse that led to fresh discussions about the future of the School site. Since the war, particularly with the establishment of GCE O and A Levels in 1951, the work of the University of Cambridge Local Examinations Syndicate had expanded greatly. Their premises in Mill Lane, built in 1885 by William Fawcett, the architect of the Perse's Gonville Place buildings, were now too cramped. Knowing of the long-held plan to rebuild the Perse at Hills Road, the syndicate wrote on 12 December 1955 to express an interest in buying the Gonville Place site.

There was a further spur at this time. The newly-founded Industrial Fund for the Advancement of Scientific Education in Schools seemed likely to make a generous grant for new laboratories, which clearly might be better spent as part of a new school than in following the second phase of expansion planned for Gonville Place in 1934.

The Governors debated the matter on 8th February 1956, considering the basic principle of whether or not to explore the possibility of a move. With one (un-named) abstention, the Governors agreed to start negotiations with the Exam Syndicate, and to mention the plan to the Local Education Authority. It was felt that the School should remain the same size for the present – a two-stream entry and a total of about 420 boys – but should be designed with the possibility of future expansion. This later became an integral part of the building plan.

Throughout the summer, negotiations continued with the Exam Syndicate, £100,000 being seen by the Governors as the sum necessary to enable a move. The nearby Roman Catholic Church, the John Hilton Bureau and Fison's Pest Control also showed interest, as did New Hall and the Technical College, but by October most had dropped out. On 27th November 1956, following an offer of £90,000 by the Examinations Syndicate, the critical meeting of the Governors took place.

Such is the way of these things, the minutes of this momentous discussion smooth over what hearsay reports as a very heated and acrimonious meeting. The record merely states that the discussions were of "great length". That there should be serious reservations about the move might at first sight seem odd. A move had long been hoped and planned for, and the teaching staff were certainly in favour of exchanging their cramped conditions for better ones. There are no earlier hints of opposition, and it would seem that it was only when the moved ceased to be a vague, long-term aspiration and became an immediate possibility that some Governors began to show anxiety.

Before looking at the arguments employed by both sides, it is worth emphasising the magnitude of the task facing Stubbs. Keith Barry, then Senior English Master, writes:

"He did not, in fact, have an easy task. The Chairman of the Governors at that time was Sir George Thomson, then Master of Corpus Christi. He was an Old Boy of the School, a previous President of the Old Persean Society, the son of the great J.J. Thomson, O.M., and himself a Nobel Laureate for Physics. For some reason he was against the move and he was, of course, a most formidable opponent. It is greatly to Stubbs's credit that he continued to press the need for change." The same point was made by a later Chairman of the Governors, Professor John Polkinghorne (O.P.), at Stubbs's Memorial Service on 4th December 1976: "The task was indeed a formidable one. I was not a Governor at the time but I can well understand the hesitations and doubts of the Governing Body. The Perse was a school without endowments other than its

*Sir George Thomson*

existing buildings. As a Direct Grant School it could attract no capital support from local or central government. The complexity of the matter and its financial difficulty were sufficient to give the bravest pause. Many Governors were hesitant, some downright opposed. The most distinguished man ever to hold the Chairmanship felt obliged to resign when his colleagues eventually agreed to go ahead. Against such odds it is astonishing that the move took place at all."

In advance of the meeting, Stubbs produced a Memorandum of his views. It considered not only the well-known defects of Gonville Place but also the question of the financial practicality of a move. This latter point was an essential one to carry. Stubbs was in no doubt.

" I believe that the present opportunity is the chance of a lifetime, unlikely to be repeated in this century, and that we cannot afford *not* to go ahead with our plans".

Certainly, pressures on the Gonville Place site had grown. If the buildings had been inadequate in the 1930s, when numbers were below 300, they were more so for a school of 421. Pressure for places had grown with the revival of the School's fortunes in the past ten years, and only three days after the Governors' meeting the *Cambridge Daily News* was to draw attention to the results of the post-war "baby-boom": in 1951 there were 10,000 children in Cambridgeshire schools, but 12,561 in 1956. It was hard to see how the Perse could continue to cope with around 420 pupils in such unsatisfactory accommodation.

*The Dining Hall at Gonville Place with the Reverend M.F. Williams supervising the Preparatory School lunch, 1950 and (below) the playground with Lensfield Road corner beyond, 1954*

The Inspection of 1951 had highlighted the problem. In a dining hall designed for 50, some 300 to 400 boys were served in three sittings. The Library, thanks to the bombing, was no more satisfactory than it had been at the 1935 inspection. The Hall still served as a Gymnasium, with no changing or shower facilities. The School faced a busy road junction which the Holford Report (Cambridge Planning Proposals 1950) showed to be one of the busiest in Cambridge, with a greater volume of buses passing than anywhere else. The Inspectors had expressed the unlikelihood of remedying the School's

difficulties on the Gonville Place site and urged the wisdom of a move as soon as possible.

After referring to this in his Memorandum, Stubbs mentioned the new pressures that threatened to erode the site, including recent road-widening schemes and requests to build a bus shelter, an electricity sub-station and a public lavatory inside the School perimeter.

Stubbs dismissed the option of expansion on the present site. He argued that it would produce "an architectural jigsaw and reduce the playground virtually to nil". In view of the Inspectors' report on overcrowding and the lack of recreational space, he could not see the Ministry of Education agreeing to such plans. In any case, he suggested, it would cost as much to tinker with the present site as to build a new school, but with one difference. There was no money to develop Gonville Place except to take out a large loan, but selling the site would bring an immediate £90,000 for rebuilding at Hills Road. The additional £50,000 he thought necessary could be met by the Industrial Fund Grant, a small increase in fees, a long-term loan and an appeal. At a cost of £140,000, they could increase accommodation by 50 per cent in entirely new buildings. He urged that the Exam Syndicate's offer be accepted.

Not everyone was convinced. The Chairman of the Finance Committee, Alderman A.A. Spalding (O.P), said he was not happy with the School's financial prospects. The other reservations are but briefly recorded in the Minute Book: that the new location would entail extra travel for some boys, and that it was important to remain near the city centre, close to the University.

When the vote was taken, eight were in favour of accepting the Syndicate's offer of £90,000. The remaining eight doubters abstained but did not vote positively against. The three Old Persean Governors were amongst them – Sir George Thomson, Alderman Spalding and Dr A.L. Peck.

The Headmaster's view inevitably has more prominence in the record of the meeting because his detailed Memorandum is included. But what of the objectors' views? We can be sure that the powerful-voiced and pugnacious Sir George, as Chairman, put his views across very emphatically. How far was he motivated by a sentimental attachment to the buildings of his own schooldays? Spalding had been a boy at Free School Lane, and his reservations were financial, but Peck, another Persean of the Rouse era, may have felt the same attachment. Recollections given at the time of Stubbs's retirement in 1969 seem to suggest that in the minds of some, the Gonville Place buildings were inseparable from "the Perse tradition" going back to the days of Rouse, and it was feared that the tradition would not survive being transplanted.

It was a view which, of course, overlooked the fact that Rouse himself had always looked to build at Hills Road. Victor Walne, Head Boy 1960-61, wrote of Stubbs in the *Old Persean Chronicle* in 1969: "Belief in the Perse tradition was the inspiration of the Headmaster's wish to provide the School with a new and much finer setting and to widen its influence". On the same occasion Frank Stubbings, an Old Persean of Rouse vintage, was similarly clear that Stubbs was in sympathy with Perse tradition, and was continuing Rouse's vision: "Thus he started early on a project which could not but attract the newest and most forward-looking of Old Perseans, but which could stir even the oldest... He has made visions reality; and he has kept the vision; and the people of the Perse have not perished".

A.L. Peck, one of the abstainers in 1956, was also eventually satisfied. As Chairman of the Governors when Stubbs retired, he wrote in *The Pelican*: "The Perse tradition, which some of us have known from the days of Rouse, has been transplanted into its new home... All Perseans, old, present, and future, must be grateful for the devotion and steadfastness which has made this possible..."

These retrospective remarks illuminate the fears that must have been felt in 1956. One governor remained unreconciled to the decision. Sir George Thomson resigned at the next meeting on 15 December 1956, when his colleagues voted 10-0 (the others abstaining) to proceed with the move. Stubbs showed strong moral courage in persisting against this formidable and distinguished man. Oddly enough, Sir George is described in the *Dictionary of National Biography* as decisive and practical, responsible for considerable development at Corpus during his Mastership (1952-1962). Yet he was unpersuaded by what, even allowing for hindsight, seem very compelling arguments for moving.

The new Chairman was the Master of Sidney Sussex, Dr David Thomson (no relation). There now followed three and a half years of exhaustive and detailed planning.

## THE CHOICE OF ARCHITECT

This was the first matter to be settled. Some sources of funding could be investigated but no appeal could be launched without a brochure illustrated with the proposed buildings. It was agreed that the chosen architect should have particular experience of designing schools and therefore of Ministry of Education regulations, and otherwise should be sympathetic to the traditions of a school nearly 350 years old. In other words, the Governors wanted modern amenities without modern brutalism.

The short list, which included Professor Leslie Martin high on it, rapidly produced an obvious choice: Stirrat Johnson-Marshall (1912-1981) was appointed within a fortnight of the beginning of the search. Andrew Derbyshire wrote of him in the D.N.B.: "If anyone could be called the

*Stirrat Johnson-Marshall*

architect of this country's achievement in building for education since the war, it must be Johnson-Marshall".

He had studied at the Liverpool School of Architecture, where he was impressed by the visit of Walter Gropius and by the idea of service to the community. After his war service, in which he escaped from Singapore and later worked on inflatable tanks and other decoys for D Day, he joined Hertfordshire County Council as Deputy County Architect, where he was responsible for eight to ten schools a year. In 1948 he became Chief Architect for the Ministry of Education and in 1956 had just accepted an invitation to partner Robert Matthew, Professor of Architecture at Edinburgh. As well as his obvious experience with school buildings, Johnson-Marshall had a reputation for imaginatively meeting users' needs, speed, and operating within tight budget constraints. It is easy to see why he was chosen.

## THE NEW SCHOOL TAKES SHAPE

"It must be confessed rather sadly that on the whole the architecture of public schools is shockingly bad". So wrote J. Rodgers in 1938 in his book *The Old Public Schools of England*. It was a tragedy, he said, that the big expansion of the public school system should have coincided with Victoria's reign. Tastes change and Victorian architecture now finds favour, but his criticisms are not without point. Much Victorian work consisted of poor adaptations of old styles. The Perse of 1890 was essentially medieval in design, centred upon a large hall open to the roof.

Since *c*.1900, however, central and local government architects had brought a new approach to the design of institutional buildings. Victorian architects were pioneers – what should a railway station, or a town hall, or a school look like? Modern buildings were clothed in the dress of earlier ages, or in bizarre mixtures of several styles, and it was some time before architects put function before decoration.

Stirrat Johnson-Marshall was, as noted above, a key figure in developing new approaches to school architecture. He was the first Head of the Architects and Buildings Branch of the Ministry of Education, whose aim was to pool knowledge and experience, and to raise the standards of school buildings throughout the country. He had met Henry Morris, the imaginative Chief Education Officer for Cambridgeshire from 1922 to 1954, who had commissioned Walter Gropius and Maxwell Fry to build Impington Village College (1936-1939), regarded as one of the best modern buildings of its time. In short, Johnson-Marshall was well versed in the best examples of Modernism, concerned with sensitive use of materials and colour, alert to nuances of light and sound, and to the effect a building would have upon its users.

Even before he was appointed, Johnson-Marshall was invited to visit the

School, on 10th January 1957. Five days later the Governors agreed to employ him. He had said that in view of the budget, a "monumental" building was not possible, but he was keen to match tradition with modernity in this the first public school to be rebuilt since the war. In March he paid a second visit to Gonville Place to look closely at the accommodation and to talk to staff.

He worked quickly. By 14th June he was ready with sketches and a model, showing the School more or less as it subsequently came to be built. The buildings were to be as close to the road as possible to reduce the cost of providing the services of water, electricity and gas. There had been a suggestion of building near Luard Road and the Rifle Range, as services were already provided there. However, it was pointed out by Hugh Percival, Senior Classics Master and for many years in charge of cricket, that this location would remove from the sportsmen the best-levelled and drained field on the site. Looking at the present immaculate

*The architect's view of the new buildings, as used in the appeal brochure*

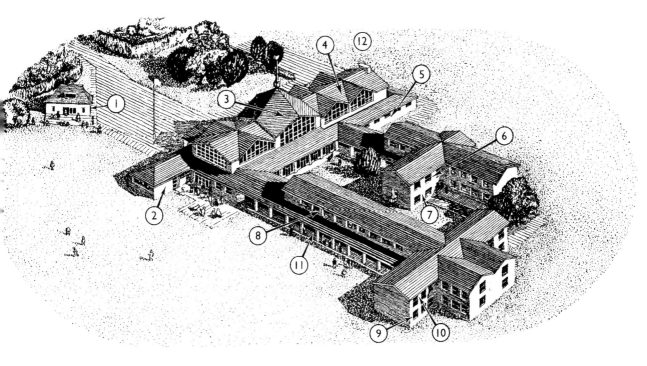

AERIAL VIEW

| | | |
|---|---|---|
| 1 Macfarlane-Grieve Pavilion (Existing) | 5 Cloakrooms | 9 Music Room |
| 2 Headmaster's Study & Administration | 6 Science Wing | 10 Mummery |
| 3 Great Hall | 7 Lecture Theatre | 11 Cloister |
| 4 Gymnasium | 8 Arts Wing | 12 Ancillary Buildings Site |

*Members of the Building Sub-Committee examine the model of the new school. The architect (right) and his assistant are standing behind Messrs Martin, Elworthy, Wilding and Stubbs*

First Eleven square we may feel grateful that this point was observed. The Building Sub-Committee agreed that a better location would be opposite the Memorial Gates, and this was the site chosen by the architect.

The design placed the Hall as the central feature, its striking timber roof being a deliberate reference to the previous roofs at Gonville Place and Free School Lane. Adjacent was the Gymnasium which could be opened up into the Hall to create a room to seat up to 900 people. Two teaching wings ran west from this, one for laboratories, the other for classrooms, creating separate Arts and Science accommodation. The alignment ensured that all classrooms faced south. The two open courts thus created were to be used for special functions only and would otherwise be ornamental and grassed. Circulation was via covered ways rather than corridors. One important aspect of the design was the potential for further extension from either wing, to create new courts in harmony with the original ones, avoiding messy or incompatible additions.

Although a large number of details were discussed right up to the official opening in 1961, there were only two fundamental concerns which needed to be resolved in the first six months. One concerned the location of the Mummery and the Music Room. The Mummery was a highly distinctive feature of the Perse which had been revived by Douglas Brown in 1949. The extensive use of drama, mime and music suggested the convenience of grouping the Mummery and Music Room near the Hall stage, where the grand piano was to be. But there were problems of soundproofing and of successfully linking the rooms to the stage. In particular, the Hall gallery and stage floor appeared to dictate a ceiling height for the rooms that was inconveniently low. In the end, the Headmaster concluded that the multiple use of the area and clash of purpose pointed the way to a separate two-storey Mummery and Music Room block – and this was added, with two re-aligned classrooms, as a small cross-wing to the Arts range.

The other chief worry concerned the Hall's "peculiar roof construction", as the Governors called it. The amount of glass seemed excessive, and doubtless too "modern". Alderman Doggett wondered about the problems of cleaning so large an area. Others raised questions about painting, sunlight control and acoustics. They particularly felt unhappy about the aesthetic appearance the façade presented eastward towards the Memorial Gates. A week or so later (this was in January 1958) the architect came back with a revised model, showing more brick and less glass, which appeared to satisfy the doubters.

*Testing the ground - Stanley Stubbs observing*

Anxieties resurfaced, however, once the Hall was up by the summer of 1959. Was it safe? Would it withstand high winds? The Governors were told that wind resistance had been calculated to 151lbs per square foot – that is to say, hurricane force. (It was tested, successfully, by the famous gale of October 1987). As for the Gallery, it was constructed to take a "live" load (i.e., with people standing on it) of 100lbs per square foot. The actual load was likely to be 30lbs, exhibiting a minimum safety factor of three, and probably greater. This may reassure present Perseans who have been known to worry about this matter.

Meanwhile, in June 1958, the contractors Rattee and Kett had been chosen to carry out the building work. They made the lowest tender (£133,857) and also offered to complete in 21 months. The ground had already been tested by Messrs Wimpey, who reported favourably: "Stiff, marly chalk, 20 feet deep". In August, the brick was chosen – for connoisseurs who might like to know, it was "Pratts" (Waterford) Light Grey. Building began forthwith.

## SCHOOL LABOURER

*TIM PLUMRIDGE, a pupil at the time, recalls working on the site.*

I have what may be a unique perspective on the building of the new Perse School at Hills Road as, in the late fifties, as a student, I worked for two summers on the site and I believe that, apart from my brother, Tony, who worked there for one summer, I was the only Perse boy to do so.

The first summer, 1958 I think, was involved mainly with foundations and brickwork. It was a beautiful summer and we all slaved away in our shorts. We worked from 8.00am to 5.00pm with a 15 minute break at 11.00am and 45 minutes for lunch. My function was to be a general dogsbody.

*Fellow workmen.*
*Tom (left) , Joe the Pole*
*(centre) and the chippie at*
*the topping-out ceremony*

One of my fellow workmen was Tom. He and I dug trenches together - at least I dug while he watched. One day we were instructed, I know not why, to dig a trench around the old Macfarlane-Grieve pavilion. We started at one corner and, after a short while, Tom suggested that we should split up and I should continue clockwise while he dug anti-clockwise. It seemed to make sense and off we went. I got to the first corner, then the second corner - no Tom in sight yet - then the third corner and there was Tom halfway down his first side. School is not the only place where one learns lessons. Another day we were sent to dig a trench to the scout hut. We had to dig up a water pipe which had been laid by some Irish contract labourers. Instead of being 2ft 6ins deep it was about 4 inches down. The pipe was a new continuous plastic type with no joints and we were warned to be very careful not to puncture it. Tom survived until about 3ft from the end when he managed to stick his pick straight through it.

Unlike today, where everything comes on pallets, all the bricks had to be unloaded by hand. We would stand there and the lorry driver would throw the bricks at us four or six at a time - very painful if you did not catch them properly. However bricks were nothing - breeze-blocks were the things that everyone hated. Not only were they very heavy but they were also extremely hot - in fact hot enough to burn you. Everyone disappeared when the breeze-block lorry arrived.

My favourite job was mixing cement with Joe the Pole. It was a quiet job as Joe never talked. I am not sure whether he could speak English but I never heard him do so. We mixed cement in a huge machine that took two bags of cement for each mix. I then delivered it around the site in a dumper truck. This was a fierce machine with a vicious clutch which made it buck alarmingly. I wondered why I was given this job as it seemed quite a soft touch - just the thing for Tom. Afterwards I found out that the previous person to drive the dumper truck had been killed when the machine turned over on top of him.

I laboured for about eight weeks during which time I was amazed how the school sprang up. We had frequent visits from Mr Stubbs but I kept out of the way when he was carrying out his inspections. I was paid the princely sum of 4/ 6d per hour (22$^1$/$_2$p for those of you who do not know the old money).

The following summer I was back again. It was even hotter than the previous summer and I got the best sun tan I have ever had. I received a pay rise of 6d bringing me up to 5/- per hour (25p) which meant I took home £10 a week - big money then.

The school had progressed dramatically during the year. Most of the bricklaying was finished but I was taught to lay bricks. Indeed the right hand gate post at the Luard Road entrance was built by me. I helped the chippies (carpenters) and the glaziers who taught me to use a saw and to glaze windows properly. I laid the insulation in the roofs and installed the guttering. I helped the foreman, I think his name was Nightingale, to put up the Fellowship boards in the gym. We put up scaffolding and were very lucky to escape unhurt when it all collapsed.

But my main job that summer was to help the man who slated the roof. My function was to carry the slates up to the roof and lay them out for him. I cannot remember his name but he came from North London and he slated the entire roof with best Welsh slates by himself. He was an extremely hard worker and I had to work furiously to keep up with him. His suntan was even better than mine.

Over the two summers I not only learnt various skills but I met many interesting characters as well. I often look at the school today and think 'I built that bit'. Some of the things that happened are best kept secret but mostly I wonder why it hasn't fallen down yet.

*Maurice Wollmann, the last Jewish housemaster*

THE BOARDING HOUSES

While the new school occupied a great deal of the Headmaster's time, he and the Governors still had other matters to consider, from the problem of finding a new Physicist to the purchase of a vegetable boiler for the kitchens. In April 1957 it had been agreed that only essential maintenance should now be carried out at Gonville Place, but Stubbs, ever active, was simultaneously looking to make progress with the last part of his development plan, the improvement of the boarding houses.

The two houses in Glebe Road had opened in 1911. They had been paid for, and run, by Dr Rouse (School House) and Mr Hersch (Hillel House), and were financially quite independent of the School. Later, however, as numbers fell, the School had taken over direct financial responsibility for both houses – School House in 1941 and Hillel House in 1948 when no Jewish Housemaster could be found. As the School's reputation revived after the war, Stubbs believed both houses could be filled and made to pay their way. Hillel House ceased to be a Jewish house and now took junior boarders. After fifty years, it was time to improve and extend the facilities.

In September 1958, Stubbs raised the prospect of an extension to the Junior House – a new playroom, dormitory, music room and better accommodation for the House Tutor – but the Governors decided it should be deferred until the finances for the new school had been settled.

Nothing daunted, four months later Stubbs returned to the issue. His plan was to add sixteen new studies to School House, a new common room and House Tutor's accommodation in a new wing that would have (incongruously) continued the line of the Middle Dormitory across the end of the tennis lawn. He estimated a total cost of £10,000 for extensions to both houses and urged this as the last part of his development scheme. (It wasn't quite the last part, as will be seen later.)

The Governors turned him down. The Junior House extension was finally built *c.*1960 but the School House extension never appeared. In June 1959 the Council of Christians and Jews wrote to ask if a Jewish House could be re-established, but the Governors felt that the difficulties which had led to them to close Hillel House in the first place still could not be surmounted, and they declined.

Stubbs considered one further possibility in 1961, that of selling the Glebe Road site and building a new boarding house on the strip of land by Long Road. This too came to nothing, though a similar (and equally abortive) proposal was made in Dr Stephen's time in 1988.

PUBLICITY AND FUNDING

The total cost of building and equipping the new school eventually came to £205,000, a good deal more than Stubbs's estimate of £140,000. As we have seen, the sale of Gonville Place produced £90,000. A further £21,000 came from the Industrial Fund, an organisation set up in 1955 by 140 firms to encourage science education in Independent and Direct Grant schools. Incidentally, it was their efficiency and the demand for a response from the Perse in two or three months, in 1956, that spurred Stubbs into pushing for a move. The Fund paid up promptly in May 1957.

A loan of £120,000 was negotiated with Barclay's Bank in March 1957 and school fees, below average for Direct Grant Schools, were raised from £60 to £64 a year. Lastly, in 1958, an Appeal for £50,000 was launched.

Keith Barry writes: "We appealed for £30,000 [*sic*, that was the original sum envisaged] and ran it ourselves, in a very amateurish fashion, for professional Appeals were not yet prevalent. The Headmaster chaired it, supported by Frank Elworthy and Frank Stubbings; and Mr Percival, Mr Hawkins and I undertook between us to write personally to every member of the Old Persean Society, with just over one thousand members at that time. Heffers printed the Appeal Brochure as their contribution, for Reuben Heffer, then head of the firm, was an Old Boy and a keen supporter of the School. We more or less succeeded in our aim, and I thought it rather fun at the time".

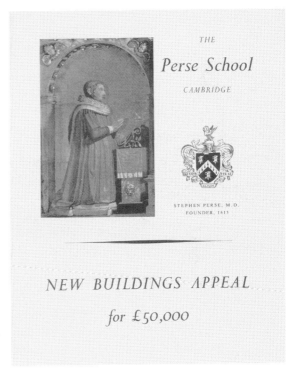

The biggest contributor, appropriately, was Gonville and Caius College, which gave £2,500. Other colleges gave anything from £10 to £500. Amongst the more mystifying contributors, at least at this distance of time, were the Evening Bridge Club, the Cambridge Allotment Society and Morley's Stores, Brixton. Premier Polish, in making their donation, must have known about all the parquet floors in the new buildings. One personal donation of exceptional generosity came from Gavin Macfarlane-Grieve, an Old Persean who was still on the teaching staff. A man of private means and a great benefactor to the School, he pledged £1,000 – a year's income for many people. Generosity is, of course, relative to one's means, and a great many people who could not afford to make a several-year covenant gave single cash donations to bring the Appeal towards its target.

Meanwhile, articles about the impending move appeared in the press, local and national. On 1 June 1957, *The Times, Daily Telegraph* and

THE TIMES SATURDAY FEBRUAR

## ARCHITECTURAL NOTES

# Complete Set of New Buildings for the Perse School

### Up-to-date Accommodation Combined with Traditional Character

#### FROM OUR ARCHITECTURAL CORRESPONDENT

It is a great many years since an architect has been faced with the task of designing a complete English public school. Many have designed additions to the conglomerations of buildings of various periods of which most public schools consist, but when new schools have been founded in recent years—Stowe and Bryanston spring immediately to mind—they have preferred to adapt existing country mansions.

One old-established public school, however, the Perse School, Cambridge, has recently taken the bold decision to furnish itself with a complete complement of new buildings on a new site, and to dispose of its old buildings. The architects for the new buildings are Robert Matthew and S. Johnson-Marshall.

#### EARLIER SITES

This will not be the first move the school has made. It was transferred from Free School Lane, Cambridge, to Hills Road in 1890, and its original site is now occupied by the university's engineering laboratories. It is to move again to a site bordering Luard Road, close to Hills Road, but about a mile away from its present site. The new site has been used by the school for playing

placed adjacent to it, so that the two can be used as a single space unified by the timber roof that covers them. Round three sides of the hall will be a gallery, which will also overlook the end of the gymnasium and serve as a spectators' vantage point when athletic events are held there.

The area of the hall under the gallery will be used as a dining-hall and will be raised above the central area to give a better view of the stage from the back and side seats when plays or concerts take place in the hall.

#### COURTYARD DESIGN

The hall will thus serve many functions, including that of a chapel, and its role as the spiritual centre of the school's life will be emphasized—and its formal character heightened—by the Fellowship board, scholarship shields, portraits, coats of arms, and other embellishments that will be transferred to it from the old buildings.

Alongside the hall will be a courtyard into which the other buildings face, rather after the fashion of the traditional college court or quadrangle. It will on occasion be the scene of social gatherings outside school hours, and the kitchens from which school meals are served in the hall have been so placed that they can also serve

The architect's model of the proposed buildings for the Perse School.

fields since 1906, and extends to 28 acres, which will give ample room for the new buildings and for the playing of games. Two boarding houses, erected in Glebe Road in 1909, are near the new site.

The present site in Hills Road, together with the buildings on it, has been bought by the university for the use of the Cambridge Local Examination Syndicate. The adaptation of the building for the syndicate is also in the hands of Messrs. Matthew and Johnson-Marshall.

#### TIMBER ROOFED HALL

In designing the new buildings for the Perse School the architects have had to provide up-to-date accommodation for 420

the courtyard and the gymnasium when these are being used as extensions of the hall.

The teaching accommodation occupies the two wings, both of two storeys, that form the long sides of the courtyard, the science laboratories being grouped on one side and the ordinary classrooms on the other. In the same wing as the classrooms are the art-room and the music-room, and above the latter is the "Mummery," a room which will perpetuate an old tradition of the Perse School involving the use of drama and mime in the teaching of English. The "Mummery" will contain a stage (with "tiring" room behind) large enough for half a class of boys, an audience

---

*Cambridge Daily News* gave official notice of the School's plans. *The Times* observed: "The School occupies a semi-island site near the centre of the City", and noted that traffic there had increased by one-fifth since 1954. On the facing page was an article on Dubrovnik, while the Commons were debating the future of East Africa – we still had an Empire then. The *Cambridge Daily News* gave details of funding. On the same day, England were struggling to avoid an innings defeat against the West Indies – so some things don't change.

Then in February 1958, *The Times* carried a large article by their Architectural Correspondent, complete with a photograph of the model of the buildings. Commenting on the boldness of the decision to rebuild entirely, the writer gave a detailed account of the plans and the thinking behind them.

The local press continued to report developments throughout 1959 as the buildings went up and the Appeal Fund grew, culminating in the topping-out ceremony of 19 July when the pelican weather vane was hoisted into place.

## UNREALISED PROPOSALS AND FINAL DETAILS

In the course of many meetings some intriguing suggestions were made, not all of which came to pass.

Early on, the Governors proposed a clock tower. This was hardly compatible with the roof design. Instead, a clock was eventually fixed to the north wall above the cloisters, facing the First Eleven square. A pelican weather vane was an obvious adornment, as one had surmounted the lantern of the old Hall. A.M. Wallis of Nottingham provided the present one.

An avenue of trees for the entrance drive was rejected, as it would have narrowed an

*Laying the drains*

already narrow vista. Several suggestions were made for the Hall. Since it would also serve as a Chapel, a stained glass window was proposed, and a light organ. Marrying stained glass to the obvious modernity of the Hall was not easy. The architect suggested the glass screen behind the stage as a possible location, but in the end the idea was dropped. The organ also did not materialise, nor did the cinema screen for which it might have been a useful partner on wet games days.

We might equally regret the absence of a swimming pool. An indoor pool 75 x 35 feet was considered, at a cost of £25,000. A technical workshop was also discussed – also in vain. Less expensive but equally abortive was the idea of a coat of arms above the entrance porch. The wooden arms above the Fellowships Board were suggested by Stubbs but it did not take much reflection to see how weathering would be a problem. A metal coat of arms was looked into, but the idea fizzled out – probably to the relief of the architect, whose clean building lines remained undecorated.

The obvious place for the Fellowships Board was the end wall of the Gymnasium, forming as it did an extension to the Hall on days like Speech Day. There were also the two War Memorial Boards, the boards recording the names of Head Boys, three portraits and 344 Honours Shields. A very satisfactory grouping proved possible, though there was space for only a selection of shields, the remainder being returned, where possible, to the Old Boys concerned. Fortunately, given the subsequent popularity of basketball, the portraits (Jeremy Taylor, Edward Palmer and Dr Rouse) were hung in the Memorial Library and the Gallery.

Accommodation for the Porter and Groundsman was originally going to be provided as flats in one of the Hills Road houses, but none came on to the market in 1957 so it was decided to build the bungalows we now have. A cedar Scout hut was purchased and the Ministry of Defence funded the CCF buildings and parade ground (note: not car park). A late detail was attended to in January 1960 when gates were made for the Luard Road entrance. Raymond Lister's firm, which had designed the Memorial Gates, produced a smaller version of the same.

One potential problem which became apparent as the buildings went up was the wind-tunnel effect of the passage between the Masters' Common Room and the Second Master's Room at the end of the cloisters. A double door was suggested as a wind-break, but the likely pressures of circulation, and the hazards of frequently opening and closing doors on a windy corner seem to have ruled this out. This may have been a matter of regret for boys who subsequently shivered there at break, waiting to see masters, but conceivably an advantage for the latter when pondering, from the comfort of the Common Room, what punishment to set errant pupils.

*The Fellowships Board in its new home and (below) showing the hazards posed by basketball until the building of the new Sports Centre in 2000*

Two slightly surreal extracts from the Governors' Minutes will serve to bring this selection to a close. The Porter's tiny room in the entrance foyer did not then have any but high, narrow windows looking out, and it was impossible to see new arrivals coming. It was suggested that a periscope be provided. And on 11 March 1959, an entry on door-handles could serve as a caption for a Glen Baxter cartoon: "Ironmongery. It was agreed that Satin Chrome Lever Handles were the only handles likely to stand up to the wear and tear imposed by a boys' school".

"OPERATION RENAISSANCE": THE MOVE, SPRING 1960

*Traditional topping-out ceremony, 9th July 1959*

The move took place in the Easter holiday of 1960, a four-week holiday to which an extra week had been added. Even so, the schedule was tight if the new school was to be ready to open on 4th May. About half of the School's existing furniture was fit for continued service in the new buildings and some of it began to be transported during the Lent Term. Vic Sederman, Arthur Hawkins and Keith Barry, meticulous organisers, masterminded the details.

In October 1956, Stubbs had bought an Army Surplus 3 ton Bedford lorry for £125, and it was in this that the School's furnishings and stores were moved. As Malcolm McFarlane, then Head of Geography, recalls: "It was driven by Mr Crane the handyman and must have saved the School thousands of pounds in removal fees". A group of eleven boys gave unstinting help, Stubbs singling out Ahmed and Bishopp for particular praise, and the Porter, MacAndrew, completed the regular team.

David Webber, who had joined the Physics Department in September 1959, wrote: "I remember helping to move science equipment…It was a rather hazardous ride as the driver was none too careful. We had to unload the equipment into what was to be the Prefects' Room because the labs were not finished. This involved driving over the building site with all its ruts. Remarkably, nothing was broken".

Incidentally, David Webber might reasonably claim to be the last member of staff to leave the old buildings. "The last event in the old buildings was not the last day of term, but the next day, which was the entrance exam. I was looking after some candidates in an upstairs room at the back of the building at the very end of the proceedings. The Caretaker thought we had finished and locked the door. Fortunately someone came round the back and I was able to call for help".

The end of the last term in Gonville Place was marked by a Thanksgiving service in Great St. Mary's Church on 28th March. When the School reassembled, it was in the new school at Hills Road.

### THE HEADMASTER'S REPORT, LENT TERM 1960

*Stubbs at his desk in Gonville Place*

At this point in the narrative it seems right to give, in his own words, Stanley Stubbs's reflections as he paused on the brink of fulfilment of a long-held dream.

"For Staff and boys alike, the last term in the old buildings was an odd one with its curiously diverse reactions to imminent change, its lack of laboratories in School and running track out of School, and its strange atmosphere of feeling for an impression. Brisk "business as usual" was rather self-consciously mixed with a somewhat faltering approach to a new way of life, and while there was little nostalgia, eagerness seemed to be curbed by a sense of unreality. There was thus a certain feeling of tension between keen anticipation and affected nonchalance but when the moment for the first lorry loads of apparatus and books arrived, there was ready help forthcoming from the Sixth Form and all worked with enthusiasm. The Old Boys at their last Annual General Meeting in the School Hall combined a natural nostalgia with a keen anticipation of the pleasures to come and there have been many congratulatory messages of good-will and congratulations from a variety of sources.

As the new buildings became more complete and their amenities more inviting, the old buildings seemed to become more and more forlorn and shoddy and when I made a last rather wistful tour of every room, I was again impressed by the obsolescence of the ordinary simple necessities of a school such as ours and profoundly thankful that the urgent recommendations in my original memorandum of 27th November, 1956 had been accepted by the Governors. I said at that time that we should be a slum in 25 years. We were very near it already. Fortune has blessed our enterprise and I am grateful. But success was also due to prudence – to most careful and meticulous planning, preparing every point of detail and investigating every need and every possible solution to an infinity of problems as they arose and all within the necessary limitations of time, space and means.

*Mrs Margaret Stubbs*

If I may permit myself a personal paragraph in this special report, for me the term has brought to a grand climax over two years of this work as described in the Building Committee's reports and it has been an arduous period. For reasons of schedules and finance and School efficiency, I have had to press constantly for great efforts and a greater sense of urgency during the whole period and particularly during this term when so many final points had to be decided, so many awkward impasses had to be overcome and so many shelved problems came relentlessly forward for equally resolute tackling. I have had the feeling of running two Schools as well as the Boarding House, one of them ideal and even ethereal with ghost boys, the other very much of this world with clamant ones. It has meant a highly concentrated effort on a wide variety of subjects for long hours. The difficulties have called for careful judgement and tact in dealing with enthusiasm, impatience, impracticabilities and temperaments, and solutions have occasionally been achieved by compromise. Progress has called for constant vigilance, drive and insistence and I have been wonderfully helped by my wife and by Mr Yates, the Bursar. He has proved ideal for the work, with a clear knowledge and calm foresight. His patient planning of detail and firm grasp of a situation have played an important part in the success of our efforts. We are delighted with what has been produced by the Architects and builders and quietly satisfied that those who use the School will enter into a goodly heritage and will quickly accept as normal what in fact represents a considerable achievement with the means at our disposal. It has been hard work and we have enjoyed it all enormously!"

*Major Yates, the Bursar*

THE VISION REALISED

"It was a wonderful first term", wrote Stubbs in his summer report. There were teething problems, of course, some trifling – the bells were not strident enough – some more irritating. The Hall and Libraries (Upper and Lower) were still not ready, necessitating improvisations for lunch and assembly for the rest of the term. Nonetheless, they were in the new School at last; they had done it.

*The Vision, 1960*

Boys, Staff and parents had been well briefed beforehand. On the first day, the arrival of the boys was staggered by one and a half hours. Each form was met by its Form Master and every boy was handed a ground plan. They were then given a tour of the new buildings and allocated bicycle racks and cloakroom hooks. So smoothly did everything run that normal timetable was resumed in the afternoon, exactly as planned.

"The impact of the new buildings on all members of the School and Staff was a stunning one", Stubbs's report continued. "There was an air of unreality about the first week, broken as it was by the Royal Wedding holiday, [Princess Alexandra married Sir Angus Ogilvy] and everyone appeared to have the feeling that this palatial setting in peaceful and beautiful playing fields with amenities which seemed lavish could not really be our home. The overwhelming impression was of quiet and calm".

The importance of a move at Easter was justified by events. A term's experience of the new buildings "with an existing and unchanged School body" rather than with a new intake of boys was of great value, especially with the "keen interest and goodwill of senior boys who would be leaving at the end of the school year".

*"SI MONUMENTUM REQUIRIS, CIRCUMSPICE"*

"It was an act of great courage to move the School", wrote John Polkinghorne later. "That it should have resulted in so fine a set of buildings is a miracle. Miracles are wrought, not by magic, but by men of vision and determination. There is no doubt that the new School is uniquely the creation of one man, Stanley Stubbs. It was his courage, his persistence, his sheer hard work which brought it about".

But of course it was also the fulfilment of a vision begun by Dr Rouse and materially advanced by him in the purchase of the Hills Road fields. When Stubbs retired, his portrait was placed in the Hall gallery. Also hanging there is the portrait of Rouse, holding in his hand a scroll of paper symbolising his plans for a new school. It is appropriate that both Headmasters are represented there, the creators and custodians of the 20th Century Perse.

It was a Stubbs tradition to start each new year with the reading from the first chapter of the Book of Joshua, beginning:

"After the death of Moses, the Lord said to Joshua the son of Nun, Moses' assistant, 'Moses my servant is dead. Now then, you and all those people, get ready to cross the Jordan River into the land which I am about to give them…'"

Fitting words for the man who carried on the work of his predecessor to its long hoped-for conclusion.

*The only known picture of the first day at the new school, 4th May 1960*

*Chapter 5*

# THE OPENING CEREMONY

The Opening Ceremony on 3rd July 1961 could not have been a happier or prouder moment for the School and for Stanley Stubbs personally. The sun shone, the new buildings were pristine after a year of final adjustments, and the royal visitor Princess Alexandra, newly-married in one of the earliest televised Royal Weddings, was perhaps the most glamorous of the Royal Family. Her dignified informality and friendly interest delighted everyone. Nearly two thousand people were meticulously ordered and stage-managed for the two-hour visit.

The Princess flew to Marshall's airport and was driven to the School to be met at the gates by the Chairman of the Governors, Dr David Thomson, the Headmaster, and their wives. The Royal Party moved towards the forecourt, applauded by the boys and guests who lined the drive. A fanfare of trumpets and the unfurling of the Union Jack were followed by an inspection of a CCF Royal Guard of Honour. Then the Governors and the architect were presented to the Princess before she signed the Visitors' Book in the Headmaster's study.

In the Hall, proceedings began with a short service of dedication, an address of welcome by the Chairman of the Governors, and a short speech by the Headmaster, paying tribute to those who had helped to make the move a reality.

"To many, planning to provide these buildings was an act of courage and declaration of faith. It is no less true that their completion is the result of great effort, of earnest endeavour, and of careful preparation. It would be invidious to attempt to name all who have played their part in accomplishing this work and they themselves would no doubt be content with this silent witness that great projects be carried through when vision and faith are followed by action, perseverance and determination.

Nevertheless, there are those whose service, encouragement and support I wish to record with warm gratitude: the Governing Body for their decision and confidence; the architects, builders and consultants whose talents were given with understanding and co-operation; the Governors' Sub-Committee – Dr Thomson, Mr Doggett and Mr Martin – who worked so hard and devoted so much

time and energy. And I must especially mention Mr Spalding, who was a boy in Free School Lane and has thus played a part in the life of each of the three buildings.

There are also those who are no longer with us, but who in spirit are surely about us and rejoice: my predecessor, Dr Rouse, who also hoped for a new school on this site; the former Master of Magdalene, Mr Alan Ramsay, who saw the distant prospect; Mr E.A. Benians, the Master of St John's, who received the 1951 Report of the Ministry of Education, whose officers gave and have continued to give great encouragement to our ambition; and Mr George Wilding, the first Chairman of the Sub-Committee, who worked so wholeheartedly and who was thrilled to see the architect's model of these buildings."

The Headmaster then invited Princess Alexandra to declare the new buildings open. She replied and unveiled the commemorative plaque now fixed to the Memorial Gates. Addressing the boys particularly, she said: "Through each one of you the influence of this historic school can contribute so much of value to the communities in which you live, and continue to realise the hopes and vision of Dr Stephen Perse more than three hundred years after its foundation."

The Head Boy, Victor Walne, then thanked the Princess before she embarked on a tour of the School. Finally, she met the staff and their wives in the marquee on the School field, before leaving to take lunch with the Governors and other guests at Sidney Sussex College (of which the Chairman was Master).

And so an idea that had surfaced in Dr Rouse's mind over fifty years before, finally came to fulfilment.

*Princess Alexandra arrives at the School, flanked by Chairman of the Governors, Dr David Thomson and the Headmaster*

*Chapter 6*

# THE NEW SCHOOL

Old Perseans will have their own views upon the merits and defects of the buildings they know so well. In this chapter we are concerned with two groups of opinion: that of the first users of the buildings, and the comments of outside observers in books and journals.

## FIRST IMPRESSIONS

*DAVID GANT was in the First Form at the time of the move. This is how he remembers the transfer from Gonville Place to Hills Road.*

### The Big Move – 1960

As I was only at the "old school" in Gonville Place for two terms, as a First-former, my memories of it are very vague. The chief general impressions are of it being cramped, dark, confusing and rather "botched" – due to the lack of specialized provision. Crowding probably led to time pressure on the limited facilities, which meant that life there seemed rather rushed. My chief specific memories, in common with almost all Old Perseans of that era, are of the Mummery. This was brilliantly improvised in a modified private residence (Pendeen House), on the school site. The way Douglas Brown made use of this building, and the quality of his teaching were unforgettable.

*The old Mummery in Pendeen House, 1950s. A scene from* Hamlet *in dance-drama*

At the end of the Lent term 1960 we cycled home from Gonville Place for

*Boys cycling in the 'pleasantly empty' drive, early 1960s*

the four week holiday; then after Easter cycled up the drive to the "new school" on Hills Road. (In those days that was the normal transport – boys being generally fitter and more independent than today). The drive then was pleasantly empty and the view of the imposing new hall an impressive introduction to our new premises. The immediate contrast was in the lightness and spaciousness of the buildings. In those days at entry there were only two Forms (60 boys) and so we all easily fitted into the Hall without needing the balconies. There was plenty of space to move about, we could play on the school fields, or could use the parade ground (completely vehicle-free). The courtyards and cloisters were a most welcome innovation, while the classrooms seemed light and airy after the dingy, poky rooms we had escaped from. I remember the distinctive smell of the rubber floors - especially for some reason in room 12. Other Old Boys have remarked on this, and 30 years on that same smell could instantly take one back in time (no need for any madeleine).

There were a variety of novel facilities:- the purpose built gym, with ropes, beams and wallbars; the science lecture room (now geography) with blinds and tiered seating; changing rooms with showers (which we actually used, rather than the modern/medieval habit of "deodorising"); the vivarium, a large pond for the biology department (now a flower bed by the concrete seat). The wash rooms were fitted with a new type of bowl-shaped urinal; I recall a friend telling me he was puzzled where the taps were.

However, what we most wanted to find out was – what was the new

*Douglas Brown in the new Mummery. David Gant sits in the second row, second from the right*

Mummery like? Pendeen House would be a hard act to follow! Here, as with the rest of the new school, we were delighted with what had been designed for us. The benches, stage, lighting, blinds, stageblocks, music box and of course the Tiring House all worked brilliantly – whilst the antique furniture for speeches had been thoughtfully brought from the old site. Sitting in my old place last summer, the Mummery virtually unchanged, I could still feel the magic of "Dougie" Brown's inspired creation 40 years on. I and a generation of Perse boys were extraordinarily lucky to have benefited from such a unique experience.

There was another effect linked with the purpose-built and spacious nature of the new school. This was in the organization of time; much careful thought had gone into the structure and pattern of the day, week, term and year – with very successful results. There was time for what needed doing, time to do things properly, without the modern sense of "diary mania". It was as though time was thought of as too valuable a commodity to be thinly spread. Most days were ordinary days, you biked to school, you had lessons, if lucky you had games in the afternoon, then you biked home. There wasn't always "something going on". ( Oh and if you think I'm rambling here, no, the sun didn't always shine – throughout March 1963 the temperature never once rose above freezing and we had no games at all that Lent term).

I thought at the time, and I still think now, that Stanley Stubbs's New Perse School was a masterpiece of design. I count myself very fortunate indeed to have been there, to have been schooled in those days, when there was less money, less consumerism, but more space and more time.

*The CCF inspection of 1963 seen from the Upper Library*

*The staff room, 1954*

*One of the Preparatory School boys lining the drive when Princess Alexandra arrived to open the School was E.J.N. BROOKES. He writes:*

"The one memory of the new school that I recall from the 1960s is that we were all so lucky to have such splendid facilities, even if certain Masters did not like the noise of the fans in the room heaters! We also enjoyed the Mummery facilities under Mr Parry. The design of the actual school hall was so awe-inspiring, as it still is, and there were uninterrupted views across the playing fields from the Library and the Cloisters, a view that is sadly gone".

*MALCOLM McFARLANE joined the School in 1948 as Head of Geography. This subject was once taught in a war-surplus hut in the garden of Pendeen House, but at the new school the Geography Room was one of the most carefully planned specialist rooms. Malcolm McFarlane's recollections begin by reminding us of the conditions at Gonville Place.*

### GONVILLE PLACE

### The Staff Room

There was a work surface along one side of the room. In the centre was a large table which could seat 8-10 people. I cannot remember there being any comfortable chairs. There was a gas ring in front of the fireplace with a kettle where coffee was brewed, and paid for, by the staff.

### Staff Cars

Stanley Stubbs had converted one of the fives courts into a garage for his car. The only other members of staff who had

cars were K. Barry and Donald Newton, who had a Triumph Roadster with a dicky seat in the back, and the Revd M.F. (Max) Williams, who came in from Cheveley.

### The School Hall

This doubled up as a gymnasium with a couple of vaulting horses which were stored under the stairs which led up to the Library. Old Perseans will remember being chased up and down by Ferdie Finch throwing a slipper at them. This was supposed to be a warming up exercise!

The lower parts of the walls were panelled and it was an interesting exercise in indoor climbing to try and traverse around the walls of the Hall without touching the floor. Getting across the doors was the main hazard and I don't think the exercise was ever achieved but it provided a challenge.

### The Dining Hall

This led off the main hall along a narrow passage. The room was decorated with photographs of the members of the School in times past, including a very young looking K.B.! Boys were sat in rows on the floor of the main Hall until they were called into the dining hall. This was very cramped with two long tables and boys seated at benches on both sides.

### Pendeen House

Was once described as best being viewed with the left eye covered and the right eye closed! It contained the Mummery and a Music Room on the first floor up a flight of steps and classrooms above. In the basement was a store for the Mummery clothes and a kitchen and a derelict room which were eventually converted into a Den for the senior Scouts. I remember evenings spent with trowel and board being shown how to plaster the walls. On one occasion the Senior Scouts conducted a fire drill, 'Escaping from a smoke filled room'. To make this realistic a waste paper basket was set alight in the fireplace of one of the classrooms upstairs. Smoke billowed out of this window in a very impressive way and the classroom smelt of smoke for several days afterwards.

### The Geography Room

This was at the back of the school at the bottom of the stairs with a view at the back over the boys' toilets. It was also distinguished by having a spring in the basement below, like much of the

*Pendeen House (one of the few remaining pictures)*

*Malcolm McFarlane in the Geography room at Gonville Place*

gravels on which this part of the town had been built. The water from this spring was channelled into a well and, from time to time, when the well filled up, a pump was turned on automatically and the water pumped into the drain outside the window. This caused an audible, pulsating sound which occurred several times a day and was a feature of teaching in this room.

### The Huts

There were three huts between Pendeen House and the Armoury building at the back of the School. The one at the back was the Scout Hut and the one at the front had been used as a woodwork room at one time but had become a general dumping ground for unwanted furniture. It was here that I discovered the showcases containing an interesting collection of fossils and rock and mineral specimens, some of which eventually found their way to the new school buildings outside the new Geography room.

*The new Staff Room, showing the work area at the back*

## THE NEW BUILDINGS

### The Staff Room

The staff were very excited at the prospect of having a room with a separate area for working. This turned out to be a bench with seating for about six people separated off from the staff room by a glass partition. The rest of the space was provided with easy chairs and coffee tables, now used as the Economics Room I believe. As usually happens the amount of books and paper accumulated soon exceeded the space available!

### The Geography Room

I was very excited at the prospect of having a specialist teaching room, the only one apart from Music, Mummery and Science labs. I spent weeks researching the needs, starting with the table size required to hold atlases and text books, and worked out that a minimum size of about 1200 square feet would be needed. At my first meeting with the architects I was told that I had been allocated 700, only 200 more than the standard classrooms. There was a small store room at the back but the result was a very crowded room as it included a wave/earth sculpture tank, which had been built to my design by Leo Sunderland, a pupil at the time. This included an ingenious adaptation of motor parts

*Malcolm McFarlane's
wave machine*

to drive a paddle which created waves, the wave length of which could be adjusted. This made possible the construction of miniature sand spit formations, as well as running water forming river features, including the effects of changing sea level. Unfortunately the leakages caused insuperable problems with water entering the cupboards below, and the tank was eventually abandoned.

## The Playing Fields

The field now occupied by the Parade Ground (Car Park) and the all weather surface was still under farm use before the new school was built. The open-air miniature rifle range was along the hedge more or less where the Sixth Form Centre and Staff Room are today. It consisted of a shallow trench with an embankment on both sides and a bank at the end where the Butts were, with a low, roofed hut to hold the firing positions.

There were no changing facilities on the field apart from the open huts around the edge of the field where the boys were expected to hang up their clothes. The staff changed in the kitchen of the Pavilion. There were no showers in the Pavilion at that time.

*The Stage and Memorial Library beyond*

*The Head Boy of the School in 1960-61 was VICTOR WALNE.*

"The challenges facing the first Head Boy on the new site, learning to manage assembly, assigning the prefects to their new duties, left little time to miss the old buildings.

Even the largely irreverent Sixth form could not fail to be impressed by the standard of craftsmanship displayed in the new buildings, by the contrasting and glowing woods, and by the superb floors laid in the multi-purpose Hall and the Gymnasium. There was some amusement that members of the staff were on public view as they took mid-morning tea and seemed nervous, when not wearing rubber soles, of climbing the circular staircase leading to the Memorial Library. Every prospect seemed to please and even the Headmaster was moved to offer a reward to the first cricketer to demolish the window of his study from the First Eleven pitch: so far as I know the offer was withdrawn before the reward could be claimed. The Mummery and Music and Art rooms were, of course, purpose built, the Trinitarian panelling and width of the Headmaster's desk on the permanent stage could not be otherwise, and only the Scout Hut did not seem, then or now, in mint condition. And the record of Open Awards gained to Oxford and Cambridge achieved that year was to stand until the early nineties."

*Stanley Stubbs at his study window*

*TONY MELVILLE succeeded Stanley Stubbs as Headmaster in 1969. Reviewing his first year at the School on Speech Day, he had this to say of the buildings:*

"This splendid hall with its ingenious use of space is an epitome of careful planning which enabled the School to renew itself... I have seen some modern buildings costing ten times as much, which still presented a somewhat mean version of themselves, not only to the outsider but also to the inhabitants. This cannot be said of the new Perse."

*In 1996, an Old Persean of the Rouse era, CYRIL ALLISTON, wrote to the Pelican with a more critical view of the external appearance of the buildings.*

"I wonder how many readers of *The Pelican* would agree that the newer buildings at the School, the Arts Block and the Margaret Stubbs buildings, are aesthetically a distinct improvement on the earlier ones? After the opening of the latter in 1961 an Old Persean remarked that he thought the designs were a mistake. When pressed for an explanation he said he suspected that there had been a mix-up and that the plans had in fact been intended for another purpose, probably a Swedish match factory. The Perse had been landed with these, while in distant Sweden a factory

*The 'Swedish match factory'*

had gone up, bearing a faintly scholastic appearance.

While not actually subscribing to this theory, I would certainly say that the earlier buildings, with all those white fascia boards, (completely out of harmony with the Memorial Gates) are at best functional. Unfortunately the 1950s and '60s were not the happiest times for school, and much other, architecture.

The big gain of course was that the School now had more room and was alongside the playing fields. But aesthetically, I venture to think, there was a loss."

Curiously, the *Pelicans* of the time contained no comment on the new buildings, only a supplement in July 1961 describing the Opening Ceremony.

PRESS REPORTS

The Press also reported the Opening but comment on the buildings was largely descriptive. So too was the article in *London John*, the house journal of the construction firm John Mowlem. In March 1961 they featured the work of Rattee and Kett at the Perse, giving particular attention to the fine and striking roof. In September, the roof was the subject of a lecture at the First International Conference on Timber Engineering, at Southampton University. R.J.M. Sutherland explained the principles involved in the construction of the whole roof canopy covering the Hall, Memorial Library and Gymnasium.

Then in 1964, *East Anglian Life* ran a two-page feature on the Perse, sub-titled "The 'New Look' of a 350 year old school". Though it carried three photographs of the new buildings, as well as engravings of Gonville Place and Free School Lane, the article was like those in the *Cambridge Daily News*, giving a short history of the School and doing little more than stating the fact of the move to new premises.

1965 saw the 350th anniversary of the School and another historical survey appeared in the *Cambridge Daily News*. In January of that year there was also a two-page article in the journal *School and College*, in

*Scene from the Mummery and (below) the Tiring House*

which CHRISTOPHER PARRY wrote about the Mummery. Parry was an Old Persean who had been taught by Douglas Brown and had now filled his post when Brown left for Reading University.

The Mummery was a unique feature of the Perse, providing a specialist classroom-theatre for boys of 11 to 13. Every detail of the new Mummery had been carefully thought out by Douglas Brown – simple, robust blackout, exposed rafters from which to hang spot-lights, a variety of blocks and steps, on the low stage, of a size and weight as to be easily moved by young boys, and all light

*The new Mummery,
The assassination
scene from
Julius Caesar*

fixtures similarly within easy reach of young hands. With eight simple bench-desks it was possible to accommodate a class of 32 – four to a bench – in only half the room. The Master had a half-sized version which in seconds could either face the class or withdraw down the central aisle to the back, facing the stage, when a performance was under way. Lighting and music was controlled from a small raised recess at the back, enabling operators to watch over the heads of the audience and to be unobtrusive in their work. The Tiring House (a dressing room and costume store) lay behind the back wall of the stage.

*Parry wrote*: "The conviction was that a room could be produced which did not require the separating of one sort of English skill, like drama or mime, from another, like free writing or formal composition, oral exercises or reading or listening, discussing poems or planning performances... The present Mummery most successfully fulfils these needs."

*Following pages:
Aerial views of the School.
Left: mid 1960s showing the new School without any additional building
Right: June 1972 showing the new Sixth Form Centre*

## CRITICAL APPRAISAL

The first critical appraisal of the new buildings came in 1964 with the publication of *Cambridge New Architecture* written by a recent Cambridge graduate, Nicholas Taylor.

The author had formed a high opinion of Stirrat Johnson-Marshall's work. Since finishing the Perse, the firm had designed the Local Examinations Syndicate building ("distinguished"), Junior and Senior Common Rooms for Selwyn College ("sophisticated") and an Assembly Hall for King's College Choir School ("excellent, well-disciplined"). This is what Taylor had to say about the Perse:

"The Perse deserves much credit for commissioning [Johnson-Marshall] to design its new buildings. His task was difficult – the total of £205,000 is astonishingly small for a school of this size. But his plan, compact and clear, is brilliantly managed, and the structure is simple and consistent. A choice of priorities had to be made, and the client expressly chose the sort of monumental timber-roofed hall which the school had at Free School Lane (1615) and Hills Road (1890). So in the central block there is a sense of transparency and space and a splendid roof. But the stage is not really suitable for drama or the dining area for lunches. Moreover, the classrooms, as a corollary, had to be severely reduced in size, and the geography and art rooms, and the changing rooms in particular, are decidedly cramped.

Within these restrictions, the craftsmanship and detailing in the classroom blocks are excellent, and the informal courts are delightful. By contrast, the hall assumes a slightly phony monumentality, with its flèche and weathercock and African hardwoods. Perhaps it mirrors the ambiguous status of the direct-grant school".

Taylor had asked Professor Nikolaus Pevsner to write a foreword to his book. Pevsner later commented on the Perse in his revised Cambridgeshire volume of the *Buildings of England* series (1970):

"Robert Matthew, Johnson-Marshall and Partners are not at their best in Cambridge…[The Perse has] completely new premises, sensible but architecturally a little weak. The main façade, behind which are hall and gymnasium, look rather temporary with their low-pitched timber gables and thin spirelet over the hall…The hall has an interesting timber construction."

But Brian Gardner, in his book *The Public Schools* (1973) was more enthusiastic:

"This is one of the most successful modern school buildings in Britain, a pleasing contrast to some of the disgracefully drab and dull blocks built elsewhere".

Much depends on one's taste. Pevsner was a Central European and a great admirer of Walter Gropius of the Bauhaus, who designed

*Page opposite:*
*Views of the School*
*from the north, west*
*and south, 1964*

*Aerial view, 1960s, from the east*

Impington Village College. But then so too was Johnson-Marshall an admirer, but he was British and perhaps more sympathetic to British vernacular tradition.

For comparison, another school building well regarded by Pevsner and Taylor is St Bede's Roman Catholic School in Birdwood Road, designed by David Roberts in 1962. Much has been achieved within stringent cost limits – like the Perse, the hall is multi-purpose (gymnasium and chapel). The low, long lines of the steel-framed redbrick building originally echoed the lines of the nearby cement works (now demolished). Or readers might care to consider the village colleges of Melbourn (1959), Comberton (1960), Cottenham (1963) and Gamlingay (1964) as examples of local school buildings contemporary with the Perse.

*To conclude this chapter, Old Persean JAMES PAYNE, currently training as an architect, gives his appreciation of the buildings.*

## THE NEW PERSE SCHOOL BUILDINGS BY ROBERT MATTHEW, JOHNSON-MARSHALL

The hugely successful architectural practice Robert Matthew, Johnson-Marshall was established in 1957 with offices in London and Edinburgh. The ubiquitous 'RumJum', as it is known, was responsible for many iconic British buildings of the 1960s such as New Zealand House and the Commonwealth Institute in London as well as universities, hospitals, airports, housing projects and power stations throughout the country. RMJM is now estimated to be one of the twenty largest architectural practices in the world, with a network of international offices.

*The Commonwealth Institute*

The commission for the new Perse buildings was one of the first commissions for Stirrat Johnson-Marshall's London office; his design team included architects who had worked with him in the Ministry of Education. Johnson-Marshall was a shrewd businessman with Whitehall contacts. His favourite catchphrase was said to be: "The right design in the right place in the right time at the right price". He was involved in the development of pre-fabricated building systems for schools at Hertfordshire County Council and the Ministry of Education. These schools were built to quickly meet the post-war needs of Britain's welfare-state schools and were internationally acknowledged for their innovation.

Architecture critic Nikolaus Pevsner, in his *Buildings of England* guide for Cambridgeshire, wrote of the Perse: '....completely new premises, sensible but architecturally a little weak. The main façade, behind which are hall and gymnasium, look rather temporary with their low-pitched timber gables and the thin spirelet over the hall. The teaching ranges are behind, low, of brick. The hall has an interesting timber construction.'

Forty years on the buildings have proved to be far from temporary and are inseparable from the identity of the School. Pevsner's comments can be seen to reflect his purist, European modern sensibility. The Scandinavian-influenced St Bede's School by David Roberts attracted his greatest praise as: '…without doubt the best post-war school in Cambridge.' I imagine the governors of the Perse considered such models inappropriate and impressed upon Johnson-Marshall the importance of the history of the School.

The new building was to continue the tradition of timber construction

*The roof and chandelier*

of the hall of Free School Lane with its hammer-beam roof. The resulting design, built on a tight budget of £205,000, reconciles this feeling for tradition with what was then the latest technology in wood construction.

The majority of the budget was spent on the main hall and gymnasium block. The hall is 50ft square with steel columns at each corner. Diamond-shaped split-trusses span from these columns to a steel connection at the apex of the roof; the interconnected nature of these split-trusses provides a wider support for the roof panels and gives the structure its pleasing prismatic nature. The trusses were fabricated on the ground from lengths of Pacific Coast hemlock with steel connections and were lifted into position with a crane. The library and gym roofs were constructed from pre-fabricated structural panels bolted together to form a folded roof construction, restrained by metal diagonal ties. The redwood boards visible on the interior of the roof plates have half-inch gaps between them to help improve acoustics.

Re-visiting the buildings recently after six years, five spent training to be an architect, I can appreciate the work invested in the design and craftsmanship. The interior of the hall is a curious mixture of the old and new. The faintly medieval wood panelling of the African hardwood

*The fold-out carrels*

*Reflected light from the pool on the underside of the gallery*

*The Gymnasium roof running into the Hall*

contrasts with the large curtain-wall glazing and the impressive cantilevered galleries. The chandelier suspended in the roof space reinforces this impression and is elegantly dated, the fold-out carrels on the gallery are ingenious but never seem to have been used. I remember in particular the reflected light from the pool on the underside of the gallery in assembly on sunny mornings (this is my madeleine!).

The form of the roof that gives the Perse its distinctive image has always struck me as being unusual and rather ambiguous in its reference, perhaps its closest resemblance being modern religious buildings. An interesting parallel can be made to The Commonwealth Institute in Kensington, designed at the same time in Johnson-Marshall's office and opened in 1962. Built to mark Britain's changing relationship with its former colonies and commitment to the Commonwealth, it was constructed with gifts from Commonwealth countries. The hyperbolic paraboloid roof spans 183 ft and is a similarly dramatic gesture clad in Zambian copper; the floors are of Nigerian timber. The interior has a similar arrangement of galleries around a central space; the building is now listed.

*The Hall from the Gallery*

*The court and
Arts wing*

The relatively high expenditure on the hall meant it had to perform several functions at once, assembly hall in the morning, dining room at lunch and performance space in the evenings; none of which it is especially suited for. Further compromises, given the limited budget, are the cramped changing rooms; several functions such as the staff room were later moved to new buildings, and initially there was no Sixth Form Centre.

The original double-crucifix of the classroom blocks forms a court, with sciences on the south and arts on the north. The traditional model of the Cambridge college is clearly an influence, typically residential accommodation arranged around courts and related to major rooms like Hall, Chapel etc. At the time of the school's construction several new Colleges were being designed in Cambridge, such as Churchill College, that reflected similar preoccupations with traditions and modernity. RMJM in fact submitted an unsuccessful scheme for the first phase of the Churchill College competition with a series of open courtyards oriented towards the playing fields along Madingley Road.

The Perse court, unlike a traditional quadrangle, was open to the playing fields to the west. In this way there was a continuous visual flow between the school and its grounds, and the main buildings were clearly visible and interrelated from all parts of the school. Unfortunately this original quality has been lost and the bulky new buildings fail to respect the original hierarchy of hall and courts established in the original plan.

The classroom blocks are of brick cross-wall construction and have

*The north Cloister*

large timber windows and finely-detailed hardwood floors on the ground floors. The field cloister to the north provides wet-weather circulation and reflects north light into the classrooms behind. Although spartan, these rooms have generously high ceilings by current standards and have adapted to many different uses over the years. Buildings today have generally higher specifications but a comparison between the school's original buildings of 1960 and the new highlight the higher standards of craftsmanship achieved by the contractors with natural materials rather than 'products'.

The Crystallographic Institute in Union Road, designed by the Danish architect Eric Sorensen is perhaps the finest building of the last ten years in Cambridge and was built with the same high standards original contractors Rattee and Kett achieved at the Perse.

The needs of the School, its staff and pupils have changed over the years and are well accommodated in the new facilities; the identity and historical memory of the school, however, remain with the Perse School as it was built forty years ago.

*Views of Gonville Place today.*
*Top left: The Cambridge University Local Examinations Syndicate*
*by Stirrat Marshall-Johnson*
*Top right: the staircase between former classrooms 1 and 2*
*Bottom left: The Catholic Church from the old orchard*
*Bottom right: The back of the 1934 Science block*

## Famous Men Stood
## Beneath This Tower

*The demolition of the
Lantern and Pelican
weathervane on the Hall.
Cambridge Daily News
28th September 1960*

## Chapter 7

# FORTY YEARS ON

### THE 1960s: STUBBS'S FINAL YEARS

The strains and responsibilities of bringing about the move took its toll. In December 1961 Stubbs informed the Governors that he and his wife could no longer continue to run School House as well as carry the burdens of the headmastership. The Governors therefore approved of Stubbs's final project, the building of a Headmaster's house in the old orchard adjoining School House. Stubbs immediately handed over School House to Keith Barry, living himself in rented accommodation until the new house was finished in 1963.

*Stanley Stubbs relaxes in his new study*

Alex Cook remarked of it: "The Headmaster's house was 'purpose designed' to provide entertainment space. However the dining room that opened from the hall and drawing room was always difficult to heat. Folding doors were fitted in the time of Dr Stephen but the draught was still great, and the dining area too small. The master bedroom was designed to have a small *en suite* facility that was fitted, from the outset, with a small hip bath. An odd choice, even for the 1950s."

*Lunch at School House*

Quite apart from the move, Stubbs had involved himself in a wide range of activities. Until 1961 he had run School House. He had continued to teach as much as possible, had taken charge of careers advice and was closely interested in the CCF and Games. For over twenty years he was a syndic of the Local Examinations Syndicate and was prominent in the local Rotary Club. He had also travelled to the United States, where he fostered improved understanding

*Stubbs teaching in the Hall at Gonville Place*

between the British and American education systems and brought the Perse to the notice of Americans who might be looking for an English school in the event of spending any time in this country. If it was felt by some that Stubbs seemed a less dynamic presence in the 1960s, it was hardly surprising for a man who had done so much and was nearing retirement.

Stubbs retired in 1969, after twenty-four years as Headmaster. Inevitably, the many tributes spoke of him as "the building Headmaster", but they also recognised that he had been more than that. As Governor John Polkinghorne wrote, "the finest blocks of classrooms will not be of much use unless the school which occupies them is running happily and effectively…It has been a great satisfaction to the Governing Body to know that the School has been in such good hands during the past twenty-four years; to see the vitality of its traditions maintained and expanded; to see its academic standards kept up and exceeded."

Former pupil Victor Walne (Head of the School 1960-61) observed that Stubbs's influence was not confined to the leading scholars, that he was anxious to see all pupils develop their talents of whatever kind, and that they should relate to the world at large and learn the value of service. "It was part of his view of education that self-confidence and achievement are not born of uniformity. Among the staff he appointed to guide us…were to be found widely differing views and outlooks and it was not surprising that education in the wider sense of the word flourished at the Perse under him."

*Stubbs and his wife with the portrait which was presented to him on his retirement*

## A. E. MELVILLE AND BENEFACTIONS OF THE EARLY 1970s

Stubbs's successor was Anthony (Tony) Melville, an Australian who had had a distinguished academic career at Sydney University and King's College Cambridge before joining the staff of Haileybury.

In the Old Persean Chronicle for October 1970, Melville wrote of his view of the future. It might be supposed that a school whose buildings were only ten years old would be well provided for. That is not how Melville saw it.

*A.E. Melville*

*The Sixth Form Centre showing how the roof lines echo those of the Hall*

"The wisdom of my predecessors and the Governing body of those times, the generosity of parents, Old Boys, and friends of the school, has provided the Perse with a splendid set of new buildings in wonderful playing fields. Nevertheless, there is much we still need. Our laboratories are small, our specialist form rooms scarcely exist, our social facilities for younger boys are primitive; we have inadequate art and music facilities and nowhere at all for boys to learn to use their hands; we lack a swimming bath, squash and fives courts; there is much in the way of modern equipment from which we could benefit. The financial problem facing any Direct Grant school under the present rules is that we are not allowed to charge fees which would, over the years, accumulate capital for building and equipment. Businesses which omitted these essential elements from their pricing policy would soon disappear. The great nineteenth century Public Schools financed a good deal of their expansion in this way, but Direct Grant schools have to reply on real asset transactions and the generosity of their friends to equip themselves for the 1970s."

The occasion of these remarks was the generous benefaction of Laurie Marsh, who had been a boarder at Hillel House in the 1940s. Success in his business career – in property, films and theatre – led him to decide that he "would like to give something back to the school which had given me so much". The Headmaster suggested a Sixth Form Centre, which was opened in 1971. Earlier in the previous year Sir John Gray, historian of the School and a distinguished colonial administrator in Africa, died at the age of eighty. He left the School some £16,000, part of which was spent on furnishing the Sixth Form Centre.

In 1974 another great benefactor and Perse character died, Gavin Macfarlane-Grieve. His

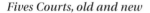
*Fives Courts, old and new*

generosity had been "almost countless". He had provided the pavilion which still stands on the School field, the School's Bluthner grand piano, fruit from his Toft estate for jam-making during the war (no small matter during wartime rationing), the bookcases to house Dr Rouse's parting gift of 3,000 books on leaving Histon Manor, and flooring for the new Mummery. His final gift was the Fives Courts, opened in 1975: he had always regretted that successors to the popular courts at Gonville Place had not been provided at the new school. They are now the only Rugby Fives courts left in Cambridge.

INDEPENDENCE AND A NEW APPEAL

In 1979 the School launched an Appeal for £175,000, the first Appeal for over twenty years. The ending of Direct Grant status in 1976 meant the end of free places previously supported by the Local Education Authority. The chief aim of the Appeal, therefore, was to provide bursaries for the newly-independent School, "to preserve the character of the School as envisaged by our founder and, in particular, our close links with Town and Gown. It is vital, both for social and academic reasons, that we should continue to select our pupils from as wide a field as possible".

Buildings came second. A new Science wing was added, and on the Arts wing, seminar rooms, music practice rooms and an extra music room were built. These additions gave more flexibility in timetabling wider syllabus choices at A level and in the provision of Science courses. The Senior Mummery, previously housed in the Scout Hut, occupied the lower room of the Science extension – though it would later have to move

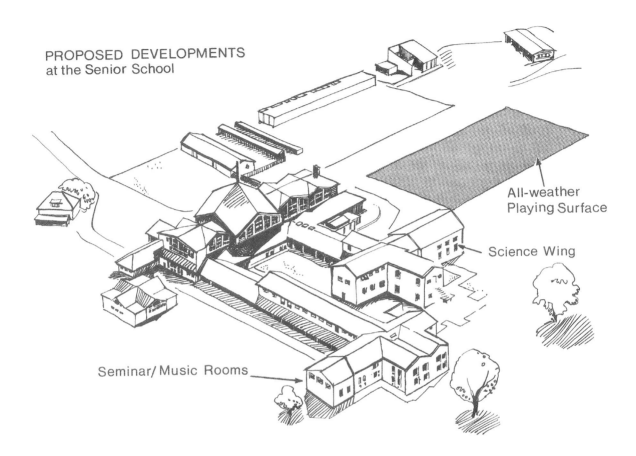

PROPOSED DEVELOPMENTS
at the Senior School

All-weather
Playing Surface

Science Wing

Seminar/Music Rooms

when the room was needed as a laboratory. The School's first all-weather playing surface heralded the growing sophistication of sporting provision in the latter part of the 20th Century. It replaced part of the South Field, which had always been the wettest and bumpiest area. At the Preparatory School, an Arts and Crafts building replaced an ageing hut.

The Appeal, professionally run but with the indefatigable Keith Barry as Appeal Director, soared beyond its target to raise £415,000 – a huge vote of confidence in the Perse and its future. Keith Barry's industry and vast range of Old Persean contacts contributed vitally to this result. Of the total, some £60,000 was invested for bursaries, as specified by a number of donors, but the bulk of the money went into buildings. The arrival of Assisted Places in the 1980s meant that the bursary fund could be built up as a safeguard against the time when a different government might choose to end the scheme.

The architects were once again Robert Matthew, Johnson-Marshall. Their extensions to the two wings of the School, although in a slightly more modern idiom, harmonised admirably with the existing brick and

*Proposals for the appeal of 1979*

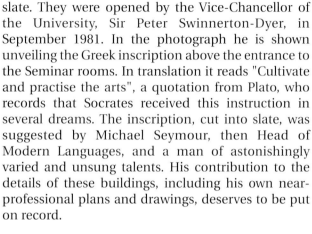

slate. They were opened by the Vice-Chancellor of the University, Sir Peter Swinnerton-Dyer, in September 1981. In the photograph he is shown unveiling the Greek inscription above the entrance to the Seminar rooms. In translation it reads "Cultivate and practise the arts", a quotation from Plato, who records that Socrates received this instruction in several dreams. The inscription, cut into slate, was suggested by Michael Seymour, then Head of Modern Languages, and a man of astonishingly varied and unsung talents. His contribution to the details of these buildings, including his own near-professional plans and drawings, deserves to be put on record.

### EXPANSION IN THE EARLY 1980s

In 1982, following the expansion of the buildings, there was a modest expansion in numbers, from 420 to 470. There were two main reasons for this. Firstly, there was competition from the newly-created (and free) sixth form colleges. Taking in new boys at 13 plus might compensate for possible losses to these colleges and thereby maintain the size of the Perse Sixth Form; but if the losses were small, the Sixth Form would grow larger and enable a wider range of courses to be offered. Secondly, class size in Forms Three to Five could be reduced. Instead of two forms of thirty in each year, three forms of twenty-six could be created by taking eighteen extra boys in the Third Form. This was a welcome reduction.

The teaching staff increased during these years from twenty-five to thirty-two, and Economics was added to the curriculum in 1984. The old Common Room was already cramped, and work facilities almost non-existent. A small extension into the flowerbeds was considered but fortunately, given the subsequent growth of numbers, a new and spacious Common Room was built. It was completed in 1984 and contained a separate workroom with individual carrels and a reprographics room. This lavish accommodation (as it seemed then) was nicknamed *The Palace* by the boys; some staff more prosaically called it *The Shed*, for it was not architecturally distinguished. Nor was it very happily sited, blocking the cloister view to the field and spoiling the North

*The Masters' Common Room built in 1984*

elevation of the original buildings. On the other hand, some felt that the Sixth Form Centre had already changed the building lines, while the need to make maximum use of the areas where planning regulations allowed building more or less dictated the site. The Staff at any rate gained a fine view of the cricket field!

Staff changing rooms were cleverly inserted on the first floor at the south end of the gymnasium, in 1982. Previous accommodation was an unbelievable Black Hole of Calcutta of walk-in cupboard dimensions, which present-day health and safety laws would condemn out of hand. Of course, in those days all masters helped to run games, and some did not deign to change at all: the donning of an overcoat and a warm hat completed their sporting costume – and advertised the level of their identification with these muddy pursuits.

The enlarged school body also required a larger kitchen, and a sizeable extension was built in 1985. These projects – the Common Room, changing rooms and kitchen – were financed by the School's own resources and the careful management of the Bursar, Major Yates, at a cost of some £250,000. This was the first such use of fee income since the Perse ceased to be bound by the Direct Grant regulations as described on page 105.

Meanwhile, the original buildings benefited from more attentive maintenance to combat certain problems that had begun to show. Alex Cook, Chairman of the Governors since 1982, recalls:

"The existence of cheap fuel [in the 1960s] meant that there was very poor roof insulation, the heat loss was considerable and the wiring gave cause for concern within fifteen years. As a result the Governors'

*Opposite:*
*Top: Michael Seymour, a leading figure in the restoration of the Ffestiniog Railway, on the occasion of his sixtieth birthday*
*Top centre: the new laboratories completed*
*Bottom centre: beginning the seminar block*
*Bottom: the opening of the seminar block*

*Unusual roof lines but awkward maintenance*

Building Committee had to plan for a considerable expenditure to rectify these deficiencies as early as the late seventies and eighties, by which time the cost of energy was rising alarmingly. In addition the large areas of white painted external woodwork were not too well seasoned, typical for the period of construction, and required frequent painting and maintenance to prevent rapid deterioration. Around the early 1980s Maurice Pleasance, a Chartered Building Surveyor, was appointed to oversee the maintenance of the buildings and, with planned maintenance, the structure and appearance of the school buildings was systematically improved."

[Maurice Pleasance has since been succeeded by Tony Nix, who has been the source of several imaginative developments.]

Tony Melville retired in 1987, having successfully steered the School from Direct Grant status to full independence without prejudice to its academic standing, and in the face of growing competition from the sixth form colleges. He had supported both scholarship and breadth in education, and this was especially apparent on Speech Days when he spoke with mordant wit about undesirable educational trends. He made sure he continued to do some teaching; it was as much a pleasure as a duty, and an invaluable way of getting to know boys and gauging their tone. "You never really know a boy until you've taught him", he said, and he knew the boys well. He saw them at their games too and was a familiar sight on the touchline in his duffle-coat and wellingtons.

In what now seem more spacious days, Melville also found time to join in the informal conversations in the Common Room – occasions when words like "Key Stage Three" or "Cross-Curricular Skills" were certainly not bandied about, but rather topics of more civilised import. Melville was a staunch defender of his staff and a punctilious observer of the proper forms of decent behaviour, notably in the hospitality he and his wife Pauline habitually extended to the Staff, their wives and the senior boys.

Under Melville, the School had weathered the "student revolt" years of the early 'seventies and the Labour Government's attack on Direct Grant Schools, had grown in numbers, and had improved its facilities through generous benefactions, careful husbanding of resources and a hugely successful Appeal. As John Tanfield wrote of him on his retirement; "He takes his place in the line of distinguished Perse Headmasters, such as George Griffith, Rouse and Stanley Stubbs, and will be remembered as one of those who played a decisive part in the history of the School".

## Dr G.M. STEPHEN: ANOTHER APPEAL

The new Headmaster was Dr Martin Stephen, a graduate of Leeds and Sheffield Universities where he studied English and History. Like Tony Melville, he had also taught at Haileybury, where he had been Housemaster of the first girls' house. He had then moved to be Second Master at Sedbergh before his appointment to the Perse. On top of his professional obligations he had found time to write a number of books, including his study of First World War poetry, *Never Such Innocence*, and had produced some notable school plays.

*Dr G.M. Stephen*

Within a year he had launched a new Appeal for £600,000 to provide a new Lecture Theatre, Art and Design studio and Modern Languages Centre in one connected block. A Sports Hall, Squash Courts and Swimming Pool also featured. In the twenty years since the planning of the new school, expectations had changed and more elaborate facilities were required. This was particularly true of the boarding houses, and an additional scheme involved selling the houses and land in Glebe Road in order to build a better-equipped boarding house on the School site. The money from the sale would also fund a Sports Hall.

The Appeal target was reached in a difficult economic period when many appeals were having little success. Keith Barry was again in evidence as Chairman of the Appeal Committee, and the first phase of development was built, including a new dining hall and kitchens for the Preparatory School. However, the Sports facilities could not yet be

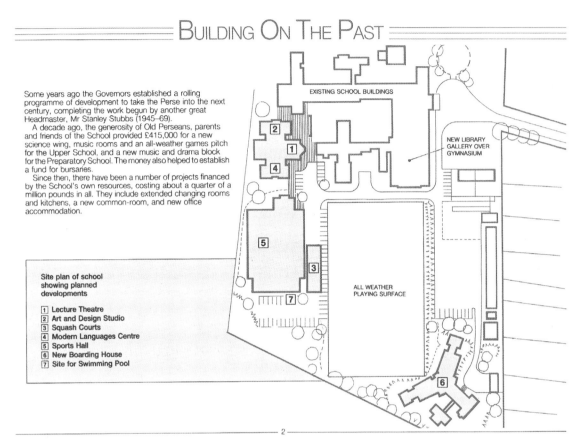

= BUILDING ON THE PAST =

Some years ago the Governors established a rolling programme of development to take the Perse into the next century, completing the work begun by another great Headmaster, Mr Stanley Stubbs (1945–69).

A decade ago, the generosity of Old Perseans, parents and friends of the School provided £415,000 for a new science wing, music rooms and an all-weather games pitch for the Upper School, and a new music and drama block for the Preparatory School. The money also helped to establish a fund for bursaries.

Since then, there have been a number of projects financed by the School's own resources, costing about a quarter of a million pounds in all. They include extended changing rooms and kitchens, a new common-room, and new office accommodation.

EXISTING SCHOOL BUILDINGS

NEW LIBRARY GALLERY OVER GYMNASIUM

ALL WEATHER PLAYING SURFACE

Site plan of school showing planned developments

1 Lecture Theatre
2 Art and Design Studio
3 Squash Courts
4 Modern Languages Centre
5 Sports Hall
6 New Boarding House
7 Site for Swimming Pool

*The plan accompanying the 1988 Appeal*

afforded. Additionally, in a change of plan, it was decided to phase out boarding altogether. Demand nationally was clearly falling and the Perse was esentially a day school without the facilities possessed by major boarding schools. The building and running expenses of a new boarding house, when examined more closely by the Governors, did not make economic sense, while considerable expenditure would have been required to improve the ageing Edwardian houses. Northwold House therefore closed in 1990 when Housemaster Tony Billinghurst retired and School House closed in 1993. The sale of the Glebe Road site was deferred, in the light of falling land prices.

Meanwhile the new range of Arts buildings began to go up in 1989. Closing the outer court, it combined three quite different buildings in a somewhat ungainly elevation. Some regretted the colour of the brickwork and the red tiles, which did not integrate at all with the existing buildings. But this was deliberate policy by the Governors, who wished for a change of style.

Nonetheless, the buildings provided much-needed facilities, while the internal decorative scheme brought interesting colour in place of safe

*The new buildings. On the left part of the Art and Design block; on the right the Modern Languages block.*

neutrality. The Lecture Theatre proved to be invaluable for a great many functions, while the new Art and Design area vastly increased the scope of work possible. The extra classrooms enabled most academic departments to have their own group of rooms rather than sharing, with a consequent improvement in subject-related wall displays. The architect was Peter Boston, chosen after submissions by six architects. The buildings were officially opened in 1991 by His Royal Highness The Prince Edward.

The other major project raised by Dr Stephen was the admission of girls into the Sixth Form. In the event it was left to his successor to implement this scheme, but the decision to admit girls was taken and a new pavilion-like building was put up to provide girls' changing facilities and lavatories. A Common Room was added in the upper storey, which would serve as a quiet work room and refuge from the increasingly crowded Sixth Form Centre, while the room below would, as Dr Stephen put it, provide a "bolt hole" in the early days, should the first girls feel at all in need of it. In the event, they did not, and integration proved very easy.

The Governors had the happy idea of naming the new building after Margaret Stubbs and she was invited to open it. Sadly, she died several months before the building was opened in May 1995. She is further commemorated by a photograph and inscription inside the building.

In 1994, Dr Stephen was appointed to be High Master of Manchester Grammar School, the first Headmaster of the Perse to move to another school for nearly a century. Apart from the Appeal he had, during his time, given particular encouragement to Art and Music, had introduced

*Dr Stephen and Mr Cook ( Chairman of the Governors) at the unveiling of the sculpture of Stephen Perse in 1994*

*The Margaret Stubbs building, 1995 (top) and the opening of the new astroturf pitch, 1995*

Business Studies, and had stabilised and kept to a trickle the number leaving for sixth form colleges. He had consciously striven to bring the School more publicity, and was helped in this by the arrival of the *Daily Telegraph* A Level league tables in 1991, in which year the Perse came ninth amongst boys' schools and was featured in a colour supplement article on the top ten schools. In this way the distinction of the Perse came to be more popularly and widely known.

## NIGEL RICHARDSON: 1994 TO THE PRESENT

As we reach the present time, this account inevitably becomes more of a chronicle than a history. It will be for later pens to give perspective to this period.

The present Headmaster, Nigel Richardson, read History at Trinity Hall, Cambridge, before spending sixteen years at Uppingham, where he became Second Master. After three years as Headmaster of the Dragon School, Oxford, the well-known preparatory school, he returned to secondary education, becoming Deputy Head and Director of Studies at King's School, Macclesfield, for two years prior to his appointment at the Perse.

*Beryl Barry opening the Margaret Stubbs building*

*Nigel Richardson and Martin Stephen in 1994*

Very early on, several building projects which were already in motion came to completion. In 1995 an astroturf pitch replaced the crumbling all-weather surface of 1980, and the Margaret Stubbs building came into use. The expansion of the Science laboratories was begun in 1996 and the long-awaited Information Technology centre was built, computers having been housed in the CCF buildings since the 1980s. The second stage of laboratory expansion came in 1997 and the third stage in 1998.

In that year, the latest appeal was launched, for £1 million. Dr Anne Lyon was the Appeal Director. The Appeal has enabled the completion of the laboratory expansion in buildings that logically develop the court or quadrangle plans of the original architect's conception of forty years ago. The Preparatory School has also acquired two new classrooms and a fine library created in a former classroom. At the time of writing, a Science/IT extension is imminent. The bursary fund has been enlarged and plans begun for an expansion of the Music School.

In addition to the Appeal, the Glebe Road site was sold, except for Northwold House, which was retained and converted into the Pelican Pre-Preparatory School. This opened in 1997 under the leadership of Mrs Penny Oates, formerly of St. Faith's School. The funds from the sale enabled the Sports Hall to be built, some ten years after the School had originally hoped to see it. It came into use in September 2000.

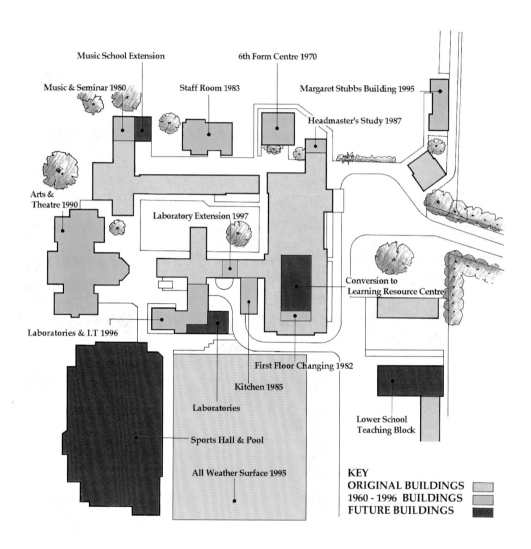

Music School Extension

Music & Seminar 1980

Staff Room 1983

6th Form Centre 1970

Margaret Stubbs Building 1995

Headmaster's Study 1987

Arts & Theatre 1990

Laboratory Extension 1997

Conversion to Learning Resource Centre

Laboratories & I.T 1996

First Floor Changing 1982

Kitchen 1985

Laboratories

Lower School Teaching Block

Sports Hall & Pool

All Weather Surface 1995

KEY
ORIGINAL BUILDINGS
1960 - 1996 BUILDINGS
FUTURE BUILDINGS

*The plan accompanying the 1998 Appeal, showing the development of the site since 1960*

The question of whether or not to build a swimming pool with its expensive maintenance costs remains in abeyance.

The Appeal and the sale of Glebe Road land were not the only sources of funding. It was early on decided to expand school numbers from *c.*480 to *c.*600 by increasing the intake both at thirteen plus and eleven plus. This has enabled a further reduction of class sizes, notably in Forms One and Two, where classes of thirty have now been consigned to history. Fees have also risen more than in previous years by an average of ten per cent a year: Perse fees had hitherto been amongst the lowest for a day school of its calibre. Bursaries and scholarships have been increased accordingly.

The result has been a larger school, a larger staff and a larger administrative staff, the latter accommodated in an enlarged administrative wing.

Not only that, the extra funding has enabled a higher level of provision of all kinds of facilities. Most notably the Library, a vital part of an academic school, has been imaginatively relocated in the former Sixth Form Centre, with scope for further expansion. The donor of the Sixth Form Centre, Laurie Marsh, kindly consented to a change of use and a new Centre was incorporated into the north end of the Sports Hall.

There have also been changes to the curriculum and to the management of the School and, after many years of discussion, Saturday morning school finally ended in 1995. But these and other matters must be left to a different and later history: our central story is that of the School's buildings and in particular the fortieth anniversary of the move to the present site.

*Artist's impression
(by Christopher Bethell,
a pupil of the School)
of the proposed
developments 1998*

## FORTY YEARS ON

Forty years on, what would an Old Boy see who once saw the buildings on that opening day in July 1961? The view up the drive is essentially unchanged, save for the traffic bumps and speed restriction signs, taller trees and different lighting – though his approach will be monitored by closed-circuit television. The Macfarlane-Grieve Pavilion is much as it was, apart from the small flat-roof extension of the 1970s.

Then he will begin to notice differences. The

Margaret Stubbs building will catch his eye on the right, as will the extended line of the administrative wing. On the left he may also notice the increased planting, clothing the bare brick of the changing rooms. If he were to move round onto the North Field he may observe how exceptionally well-kept is the cricket field, the result of the skilful work of the devoted and long-serving groundsman Doug Collard and his staff. He will see the Sixth Form Centre (now Library) and Masters' Common Room. Future building here will close off the cloister view of the field, but Tony Nix's imaginative plan to extend the Library by replicating the novel lines of the former Sixth Form Centre will do much to restore harmony to this northern elevation.

When he moves round towards the South Field he will see the biggest changes and realise that the area of the School buildings has virtually doubled in forty years. There is the Arts and Theatre range in its contrasting orange brick, and beyond it the pale yellow brick of the huge Sports Hall. Walking towards the inner courts he will find the new laboratories and Information Technology wing creating two new open courts in the style and brick matching that of the 1960s. We may venture to think that he will be struck by the quality of the landscaping and planting that has occurred, much of it the enthusiastic labour of love by a member of the Common Room. He will also see new paths across the courts and a new archway where the old Prefects' Room used to be, to accommodate the increased traffic between the original part of the School and the new additions on the south west of the site.

Inside the new buildings he will encounter rooms appointed to a standard undreamt of forty years ago, but if he looks into the old rooms he will find them wearing extremely well, even if their parquet floors are now carpeted. Indeed, the buildings and grounds are now maintained to a higher standard than ever before, under the eye of a recently-appointed Estates Manager.

In all the changes of the past forty years, however, it is still what the Chairman of the

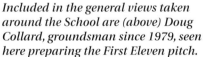

*Included in the general views taken around the School are (above) Doug Collard, groundsman since 1979, seen here preparing the First Eleven pitch.*

*The picture of the Hall interior (immediate right) shows the portraits of Rouse and Stubbs whose vision led to the building of the present School, and (below right) a watercolour of the new Sixth Form Centre by Keith Hornblower*

Governors calls "the visual impact and unique design of the hall and its roofline" which remains the timeless architectural embodiment of the Perse, echoing and transforming the hall of Gonville Place, and the original hall of Free School Lane, where the school began nearly 400 years ago.

*Aerial photograph from the late 1990s (compare to page 91)*

*Chapter 8*

# MEMORIES

*In the final chapter, Old Perseans look back and convey their impressions of the Perse in each decade from the 1950s to the present.*

**THE PERSE IN THE 1950s**

*By VICTOR WALNE – Head of the School 1960-1961*

As well as his commitment to the tradition of independent education of which he becomes both interpreter and guardian, every Headmaster of the Perse embodies the spirit of his age. If the Forties are now remembered for heroism and austerity and the Sixties for hedonism and audacity, the Fifties, in retrospect, seem remarkable only for the virtues of progress and continuity. Having come to terms with post-war economic realities, Britain was gradually gaining confidence in a new role in world affairs, which nevertheless continued to give expression to many old concerns. In 1959 a populist Prime Minister in patrician disguise claimed electoral victory with an advertising slogan "you have never had it so good", referring to an increasing supply of television sets, washing machines and the new Mini. These new consumer values would not have been approved of by Dr Rouse. In some contrast, the early years of the decade had reflected a national mood in favour of returning to an imagined pre-war normality of railway porters, policemen on bicycles, the Third programme and a sense of public duty. But the changes brought about by the 1944 Education Act, which encouraged the rise of a meritocracy in a world declared open to social mobility, were intended to be irreversible. The new social and educational order was symbolised by the Direct Grant schools, of which the Perse was one and, in comparison, much smaller than most. The architect of the 1944 Act later became, as Lord Butler of Saffron Walden, Patron of a School Appeal. Stanley Stubbs, meanwhile, was quietly engaged in judging when the time would be right to move the Perse to a new site. The new buildings, first occupied in 1960 but opened in 1961, were themselves a monument to conservative optimism and perfectly expressed the progress and continuity which Mr Stubbs also made the hallmark of his Headmastership.

The Direct Grant Schools were expected to produce results, building on selection at 11+ and the subsequent award of scholarships through State funding. The Headmaster, however, cherished the Perse tradition

*The Fellowships Board,*
*Gonville Place, in the 1950s*

as a gift to be passed on to every boy in the School, whether or not he had won a scholarship there. He impressed on the new arrival at the Perse that he had been judged worthy of a place, was himself a link between past and present, and was accepting obligations which the Headmaster would recall to his mind whenever necessary. Referring regularly to the public school ethos, which was expressed in a variety of ways, including a requirement to wear School caps on passing prefects on gate duty, Mr Stubbs did not allow the reality to be hidden that every school lives by a regime. the Perse tradition of academic excellence was upheld by the Fellowships Board underneath which he sat in Assembly, and which was, as he pointed out, amongst independent schools a unique record of elections mainly to Oxford and Cambridge Colleges since the School's foundation in 1615. Having in mind, no doubt, the sacrifices of two World Wars recorded by the names of Old Perseans on the Memorial Boards in the old Hall, as well as the School's reputation for educational excellence, Mr Stubbs seemed sometimes to live in an Olympian detachment from the day to day lives of boys for whose future he had accepted a considerable responsibility. Even boys who were late for school after doing a paper round, and had to report to him personally could, however, be pleasantly surprised by his extraordinary directness and courtesy.

Certainly in the Fifties, and notwithstanding Mr Stubbs' personal recommendation of the benefits of character in industrial management, academic values set the tone at the Perse and served to establish the career choice of many pupils. But, at the same time, they divided the academic sheep from the non-academic goats, leaving neither party in any doubt about its status. The Headmaster also showed little understanding of those whose temperaments caused them to resist the demands of conformity. Praise, on the other hand, was an essential part of school life, and was freely given to boys who, in whatever way they chose, or were best suited for, committed themselves to the opportunities provided for them. Perhaps the public school ethos was upheld more vigorously in the lives of the boarders than the day boys. The reality was that the Perse was not well endowed, kept fees low and no one thought of cachet. More importantly, the Perse tradition had attracted to the School throughout the 20th Century a staff of quite remarkable teaching abilities and of which Mr Stubbs was, in the main, a very good judge. Amongst boys and staff were to be found widely different outlooks. Not surprisingly, education in a wider sense of the meaning of the word than the 1944 Act seemed to look for, flourished at the Perse School under his Headmastership.

It was part of Mr Stubbs's philosophy of education, and belief above all in the value of giving service, that self-confidence and confidence in others are not born solely of intellectual gifts. In comparison, however, with one in three now, only one in ten school leavers in the Fifties could be offered a University place and boys with an ambition to excel, and there were many at the Perse, had also to be examination-conscious. The streamlining of educational progression obliged boys, even at the Perse, to choose in their third year between Greek, German and Science, as "O" Level subjects which would also predetermine their choices at "A" Level. As a condition of university entrance, every boy pursued Mathematics (including a Further Maths option), Latin and French to his fifth year in top, bottom or for Maths third sets. On the new site, provision of extra laboratory space at last made possible the end of this premature bifurcation of intellectual interests and career paths. As evidenced by the shields hanging in the old Hall, recalling the examination successes of the servants of an Empire, competitive examinations were nothing new. But the new meritocratic principles were, on the one hand, re-inforced by public examination at "Ordinary" and "Advanced" levels in up to ten and up to four subjects respectively. And, on the other hand, well into the Fifties, public examinations also supported the surviving vitality of a classical and humanist belief in the importance of service to the State. There were then few opportunities, through gap years, extra-curricular activities and encounters with adults, to find expression either for qualities of personal enterprise or for community service.

*Walking from the Gonville Place common room are, from left to right, Malcolm McFarlane, John Tanfield, Keith Symons and Vic Sederman, 1954*

Members of the staff, each one playing to his considerable personal strengths and of course always wearing gowns for Assembly and in the classroom, worked well in subject teams and many would remain at the Perse for their entire careers (Mr Hawkins, Mr Barry, Mr Percival, Mr Tanfield, Mr Sederman, Mr Mitchell, Mr McFarlane, Mr Billinghurst, Mr Webber and Mr Seymour amongst them). Although, for fourth and fifth formers, a sense of pressure, which returned again in the "A" level years, developed as "O" level syllabuses (now known as subject specifications) were embarked on, boys at the Perse, more aware of dealing with personalities than with a system, knew they were in good hands. Habits of disciplined work were duly formed. A patient (normally) and systematic (invariably) approach by the Staff to their task demanded and got (not surprisingly) the best that boys could give. As the Senior English Master (Keith Barry) remarked, when Maurice Wollman retired to compile anthologies of prose and verse, almost no-one he taught ever succeeded in failing English "O" level. Academic results in 1959 and 1960 were to be remarkable. In 1960, nine boys gained Open Awards at Oxford or Cambridge Universities in English (2), History (1), Classics (1) and the Sciences (4). Peter Lapwood was tragically killed in a bicycle accident

*John Clarke in 1961, with Princess Alexandra*

*F.R. Leavis c.1913*

before being able to take up a Major Scholarship in Mathematics at St John's College Cambridge. Within a couple of years, from a small Sixth Form, five leavers from the Science Sixth, Christopher Redman, David Thomas, Ed Shire, John Clarke (a future FRS) and Brian Bertram (to succeed Sir Peter Scott as Director of the Wildfowl Trust at Slimbridge) went on to distinguish themselves, four as Professors. In 1960-61 Old Perseans were appointed Director of the Royal Shakespeare Memorial Theatre (Sir Peter Hall), Principal of the Royal College of Music (Sir Keith Faulkner), President of the British Association (Sir George Thomson) and Director of the Geological Survey of Great Britain (Dr C.J. Stubblefield).

In the Fifties, any link between science and the performance of the economy was hardly acknowledged and an elitist distinction between pure and applied was uncompromisingly upheld by Mr F.C. Brown. In the days before the discovery of DNA, and the Electron Microscope, the development of computer technology in earnest and the launching of the Hubble telescope, scientists were popularly still known as boffins. Boffins were expected to busy themselves as inventors working within a Heath Robinson framework as immortalised in the cartoons of Ronald Searle. Although it was already clear to Perse boys in the Fifties that Science might open up as many career opportunities in the future as Classics had done in the past, it still surprised no one when the brightest boys chose, with an eye to an Open Award at Oxford or Cambridge Universities, to study Classics under the able tutelage of Hugh Percival. The Sciences had, however, never been neglected by a school which, by the middle of the 20th century had produced two Nobel Prize winners, one of whom, Sir George Thomson, was serving as Chairman of the Governors; and four Fellows of the Royal Society. But unmistakably, in the company of Mathematics, the Sciences were beginning their ascent to the virtual curricular hegemony they would achieve by the end of the century, when Governments would be calling for the curriculum to be more broadly based. Another Old Persean, the great literary critic Dr F.R. Leavis, (subsequently Companion of Honour) also rose to national prominence as a protagonist in a famous debate about the existence of two cultures, the humanist and the scientific.

The cultural life of the Perse in the Fifties was, indeed, humanist, at least in inspiration, extolling the supremacy of the spoken word made famous, through the medium of the Greek and Latin languages, and as an education of the elite, by Dr Rouse. To the fore were the histrionic arts of oratory – the whole School would assemble in the Hall for Orations – drama, mime, poetics and debate. Not being part of the culture of the spoken word, neither Art nor Music found a proper expression in the formal curriculum but the personal commitment of members of staff, and above all of Douglas Brown (O.P.), ensured that Music did do so in School life. Shortly before his early death, Douglas Brown occupied a Chair of Music and English created for him at York

University to which Dr F.R. Leavis succeeded. The Musical Society, however, struggled against the odds. Mr Stubbs did not find time to receive Imogen, the widow of Gustav Holst on a visit to the Perse. If much of the best teaching took place in Pendeen House, a structure which seemed to everyone to have passed its demolish-by date, and was the home of both the Mummery and the Music Room, the cultural triumphs of the decade were celebrated in the Hall.

The dramatic and musical entertainment presented there were not, however, in the Music Hall tradition. On the contrary, in the Hall the Perse community was reminded of (a view also expressed post-war by Dr Leavis and T.S. Eliot), Dr Rouse's belief that the best is the prerogative of the few. Mr Tanfield's direction of the Perse Players, which earned him a caricature in Punch magazine, helped to lead a national revival of Shakespeare's plays after the War; and was linked to the Royal Shakespeare Company in the person of Peter Hall (OP), who as Hamlet, had reduced some

*The cast of* Hamlet *in 1949. Peter Hall in black (centre), John Tanfield two places to his right*

of his audience in the Hall to tears. Peter Hall sent first night good wishes to the Players throughout the Fifties. the Perse Friends of Music, another vehicle for Douglas Brown's exceptional talents, arranged for concert pianist Peter Katin to play in the Hall, at an early stage in his career as an exponent of Chopin and Liszt. Douglas's talents as a librettist were revealed in Scouts and Sports Concerts which gave expression to the lighter side of school life as well as to the talents of the boys who preferred not to audition for the Perse Players. Douglas's production of the *Song of Hiawatha* attracted a capacity audience to the School.

The School's religious ethos in the Fifties could be described as broad church. Boys were expected in Assembly to sing from the Public Schools Hymn Book. Malcolm McFarlane undertook preparation for the GCE "O" level examination in Religious Knowledge, offset by Mr Macfarlane-Grieve's excursions into comparative religion. Their work, and the contribution of low-key organisations such as the Crusaders, ensured that the fashionable muscular Christianity made no headway at the Perse. Jewish boarders, and a very few Catholic boys withdrawn from Anglican worship by their parents, were supervised by Maurice

*Hillel House, 1918, with Mr Hersch, the first housemaster*

Wollman until the end of Assembly in the Hall. The Jewish presence at the Perse, one of the only two independent schools to have had a Jewish House, seemed to be an entirely unremarkable aspect of School life and simply reflected the School's tolerant and comprehensive approach, the legacy of Dr Rouse, to religious and philosophical commitment and diversity. the Perse still possesses a unique and, from the point of view of Anglo-Judaism, an important photographic record of the life of the Jewish boarders, which deserves its own gallery.

Of course, awareness, spontaneity and curiosity were the natural by-products of good teaching and would no doubt have been enough to preserve the Perse from the obsessions revealed in their memoirs by some notable writers recalling unhappy experiences of boarding school life in rural fastnesses. Nevertheless, the public school ethos and its traditional emphasis on team spirit and sporting prowess was duly maintained at the Perse in the hierarchical panoply of Pelican and School colours: Major and Minor Sports, Captains and Vice-Captains, First and Second Fifteens and Elevens, Colts and Minor Colts and the league of Uncommitted who were banished to the remoter corners of the Playing Fields. Memories of school life in the Fifties will, therefore, be coloured or shaded by the demands made on boys on Tuesday and Thursday afternoons throughout the year. In their first term, new boys were, for purposes of developing their team spirit, recruited at a sort of School auction into East, West, North and South (for boarders) Houses, with more of a show of solidarity than of sporting intent: whereafter they were expected to play up, play well and play to win, which many did. All boys were regularly required to run round a small or large triangle of roads to the south of the Field, an exertion which by no means made impossible some enjoyable conversations in winter sunshine. Following, or so it seemed, the natural cycle of medieval agriculture, Rugby was played in the Autumn, Hockey in the Spring and Cricket and Tennis in the Summer terms, with the Uncommitted lying fallow as well as out of sight.

On moving to the new site, Mr Stubbs offered to reward the first cricketer to demolish the very large picture window in his study which overlooked both the First Eleven pitch and his rose garden. Feeling slighted, the Tennis Six fell to considering how to demolish rather more than the window. Neither has yet come to anything; but it is rumoured that Mr Richardson, occupying only half the space in his study available to Mr Stubbs and presenting only half the risk, has taken out a general accident policy on favourable terms. Naturally, and as examples of *mens sana in corpore sano*, most members of the Staff were as expertly engaged on the Playing Field as they had been in the classroom, helping boys to find their level, and some boys to excel, in their chosen sport(s) as well as subject(s). Training sessions were offered and taken advantage of; proper circuit training was only possible on the new site. Results were read out at the end of Assembly as was the conferment of School Colours. Records were meticulously kept. A competitive swimming event was held annually in the municipal pool at Jesus Green and a Sports (Athletics) Day at Fenners, followed by an annual Sports Concert in the Hall. Gymnastics, however, was not well catered for. Perseans of the Fifties will recall avoiding Mr Finch's bomb, a plimsoll launched by him around the old Hall on dangerous trajectories. Mr Finch's Naval background also made him an ideal Swimming and Boxing instructor.

Boxing, however, was beginning to be seen as potentially dangerous and did not survive the move to the Hills Road site; the Perse is still without a swimming pool, even as the River Cam in its unpredictable depths still flows past where the Swimming Sheds used to be, and in the evening of his life, Mr Finch became a familiar figure in the public houses of King Street. Away from public gaze, impromptu games of soccer took place on most days in the playground, blazers and caps defining goalposts. They too have been lost in the mellow mists and memories of a Cambridge autumn. On the Gonville Place site distances were short. At the end of a lesson, if you sat by the door in most classrooms, you could make it to the Fives Courts in under 20 seconds and to the head of the biscuit queue in under seven. Neither Fives Courts nor the biscuit queue made it to the new site.

It is not surprising that on the Gonville Place site an almost immediate

*Browsing in the Library*

sense of familiarity drove out any sense of confinement. The first buildings there reflected the influence of the architecture of Norman Shaw and his vision of "Olden England", as did the Catholic Rectory opposite. The subsequent Science Block built in 1934, Army Huts to house the Scouts and the Bicycle Sheds reflected more utilitarian pressures. The external appearance of the School Hall had a well weathered and welcoming appeal, as well as the dignity of architecture of the high Victorian epoch, in which Dr Rouse, possessing the qualities himself, must have felt very much at home. Outside lessons, of course, and as a rule not into the Orchard, boys were free to roam about the Hall and the site as they wished. Lunchtime ruminants, now browsing in the Library, might be able to listen to Cecil Crouch play Strauss or Rachmaninov on the grand piano. At lunchtime, Douglas Brown, who had succeeded Caldwell Cook in the School's famous Play Way tradition, sometimes arranged gramophone record concerts in the Mummery.

In the Fifties, Douglas Brown was at the height of his teaching powers and in the Mummery, which lacked the formalities of both classroom and theatre, the task of teaching First and Second Formers to express themselves in the spoken word, so central to the Perse tradition, was, at best, turned into a personal adventure of poetic and dramatic discovery. Douglas, in the Mummery, had both a formidable and reticent presence, somehow being able to combine encouragement and expectation with the disciplined attention required for play or poetry readings, costume dramas such as Philoctetes and, of course, mime. The Mummery experience lay both inside and outside School life and Douglas had a conscientious concern for able boys who were stumbling over public school ethos. The Mummery also provided a stepping stone to membership of the Perse Players and a foundation on which Keith Barry and Maurice Wollman subsequently built knowledge of the skills required for passing the English "O" level examination. In the Sixth Form, picking up the threads of teaching again, Douglas attracted many boys to study English for University entrance. Rarely were he and his scholars (including Christopher Parry and David Roulinson, who were to return to the Perse as his successors) seen carrying fewer than four books each about School.

The Music Room was equipped with an upright piano and a record player. In the Fifties musical instruments were rarely in evidence. Mr Macfarlane-Grieve will be remembered for his unavailing efforts to persuade boys to sing along with him to Purcell and Tallis: but in the

Music Room the back row always filled first. Pop music was growing past its infancy and boys, not realising that pop music was mainly a commercial phenomenon, were learning a new vocabulary of record albums, hit singles, backing groups and vocalists. The boy who brought into school a long-playing record from America of the "rock idol" Elvis Presley became an instant celebrity. This new phenomenon would emerge fully-fledged with The Beatles. Traditional cultural mores were being undermined in other directions too, through advertising agencies and media empires. Radio performances by The Goons were eagerly anticipated and rapturously recalled by many Perseans of the Fifties and, indeed, by the heir to the throne himself. *O tempora, O mores!*

Uniforms were a permanent requirement of life at the Perse and Prefects' boaters may still be glimpsed on the croquet lawns of some Cambridge Colleges. A Combined Cadet Force (CCF) paraded on Monday afternoons under the commands of Major Stanley Mitchell (Army), Lieutenant Commander K.N. Symons (Navy) and Flight Lieutenant Victor Sederman (RAF) for drilling and sectional activities. Appearing in cap and gown on ceremonial occasions, Stanley Stubbs was a firm supporter of the virtues of discipline, self-reliance and service to the State, which he believed the CCF developed. Guards of Honour were drawn up for important visitors. Members of the CCF could also look forward to field days, practice on the rifle range, regattas on the Norfolk Broads, overnight visits to a variety of installations and even airborne hops in a glider on the Playing Field. In the Fifties, the CCF prepared boys for their National Service; but the divisive Suez adventure, and wars of attrition or confrontation in Cyprus and Malaya, revealed both the logistical problems of moving about Britain's limited military resources and the need for more professionalism in the Services. As a consequence, National Service was abolished in 1958.

The Scouts wore the uniforms of the 5th Cambridge troop with special pride. Douglas Brown was an inspired interpreter of Lord Baden-Powell's "Scouting for Boys" and was supported by a remarkable team of volunteers. Like the Headmaster, but with a different social vision, Douglas strongly believed in leadership qualities. Each year Arthur Hawkins (Second Master and deputy for Mr Stubbs during his absences in America), Ferdy Finch and Uncle Mac (Mr Macfarlane-Grieve) from the staff and recent old boys, including Colin Cope and David Loades, lent their administrative talents for the Annual Scout Camp at West Runton on the Norfolk Coast. A full day might begin at sunrise with a solitary walk on Cromer Sands. Douglas frequently rehearsed Lord Baden-Powell's remark that most of the day's work could be done before 7.00am. The day would also encompass adventure activities in the woods above the camps, cooking on open fires, and practising First Aid before the evening's entertainment, and prayers, around the Camp Fire. How much in practical and spiritual ways could be learned from Scouting at the Perse in the Fifties only members of the troop will ever

*CCF Inspection 1962. Stubbs with Stanley Mitchell behind*

know. It was primarily as Scout Leader that Douglas was also able successfully to integrate his traumatic personal experiences as a medical orderly in the War into his professional life, to the great benefit of all who were fortunate enough to be taught by him.

Douglas Brown and John Tanfield provided teaching of the highest possible quality throughout the Fifties at the Perse. Mr Tanfield captured, and held, the attention of his class with a pedagogic tour de force, combining a didactic flow of narrative and analysis with a dramatic flourish (which some unfortunate boys encountered personally) and an unanswerable Parthian shot. Mr Tanfield's teaching methods rendered the reading of history books largely superfluous, but he always recommended this diversion to his class. David Loades was one of Mr Tanfield's earliest pupils and Harold James one of his last, both becoming distinguished Professors of History at the Universities of Wales and Princeton respectively. Eccentric in some habits, John Tanfield moved quickly about the School buildings, close to walls and radiators, wearing his gown so loosely that it swept dust from the floors onto its fabric and was gradually shredding itself on the obstacles it encountered. No one cared to bet on anything about Mr Tanfield: but there were those who thought his gown would not survive the move to Hills Road. They were wrong. Before the connection between ill health and cigarette smoking was established both Mr Stubbs (Passing Clouds) and Mr Tanfield (Woodbines) were regular smokers. Mr Symons and

*The Common Room, Gonville Place. From the left: H.G. Taylor (the Bursar), H.E. Percival, J. Buchanan, F.C. Brown and C.W. Crouch*

Mr F.C. Brown smoked pipes, in the former case impressively setting off his Naval Uniform and in the latter his sartorial preference for Plus Fours. [The School is now a non-smoking site!] Most members of the Fifties Staff were well turned out. At election times, Mr Percival, who served as Chairman of the Cambridge City Labour Party, wore a red tie. Although he denied his tie had any significance, the first post-war Labour M.P. for Cambridge had sent his son to the Perse. Mr Stubbs drove to school in a modest Standard Vanguard. Mr Barry and Mr Symons both arrived in the sort of sports car that challenged the austerity of the times, whilst almost everyone else came on bicycles, Douglas Brown's being motor-assisted.

The Perse in the Fifties worked extremely well both as a community of its own and as part of the wider Cambridge community. Most of the Direct Grant schools drew pupils from urban catchment areas, and the Perse was expected to be, or to continue to be, a permanent link between town and gown. Dr Rouse had been made an Honorary Fellow of Christ's College: most Headmasters of the Perse were Cambridge graduates, as were in the Fifties many members of the Staff: and the Chairman of the Governors was also Master of Corpus Christi College. In the days before more prosperous times allowed for the extension of University building on any scale, University representatives on the Governing Body, working in similar conditions themselves, seemed unaware that cramped premises (and limited scope on the Gonville Place site for expansion) could scarcely contain the energy, creativity and ambition for which the Fifties at the Perse deserve to be remembered.

Mr Stubbs knew that rising building costs might pre-empt a properly-considered decision whether or not to move the School to the magnificent Hills Road site it already owned. The School's future security, and capacity to respond to a demand for places, depended on a willingness to take a present risk for which he was well prepared. Significantly enough, a grant from the Industrial Fund to build new science laboratories decisively underwrote the School's finances. The inspiration, however, of his wish to provide the School with a new and much finer setting, and to widen its influence, lay firmly in Stanley Stubbs' belief in the Perse tradition of which his visits to the United States had, if anything, made him more

*Letters to Mr Stubbs from around the World*

aware. He was also fortunate. If the spirit of the age had been reactive, or if its different elements had been irreconcilable, any Headmaster's task would have been extremely difficult. the Perse tradition, and everything he achieved for it, was celebrated at the Royal Opening of the new buildings, the Perse being the first independent school to rebuild completely after the War. In planning the Opening Day, and every second of the Royal presence in the School (and it should be added the HRH Princess Alexandra of Kent wanted to see everything) he revealed his sense of historic occasions as well as his enjoyment of them. Mr Stubbs told me as his Head Boy, during a rehearsal of the Royal Opening, that he wished to be remembered as the building Headmaster. I thought then, and forty years later I still think, that was too modest a wish.

### THE PERSE SCHOOL IN THE 1960s: A PERSONAL VIEW

*By DAVID UTTING*

Even while they were still 'happening', the Sixties were trumpeted as a decade of cultural upheaval. Young people were so much to the fore in many of the characteristic challenges to authority and convention that occurred that it is unlikely that the Perse School could have avoided change if it had wanted to do so. Yet any idea of a school in the continual throes of turbulence would be spectacularly misleading. My schooldays were stimulating, mostly enjoyable and included some moments of dismay and excitement; but they were much too placid to match the media's retrospective stereotypes of rebellion and licentiousness.

The fact that I was only seven years old when I entered the Prep in 1960 is one self-explanatory reason why so few memories relate to the supposed Sixties mantra of 'sex, drugs and rock and roll'. (Readers disappointed by this admission should move quickly to the penultimate paragraph). As a member of Miss Carmichael's anachronistically-numbered Form 2, I attended the opening of the new Upper School, and sat cross-legged beside the driveway as Princess Alexandra's car drove past. But at that age, modern architecture was less intriguing than the Prep's Victorian house, assorted huts and its wooded grounds with important den-making potential. The state of sustained happiness that I associate with that time relates mostly to the staff who worked there under the friendly, though superficially gruff, leadership of Hugh Lindeman. I might now speculate on how far Froebel Institute training explained the quality of teaching, but as a child I knew that learning had become a joy and an adventure. We stormed through the 'three rs'. But with teachers of the calibre of Bridget Carmichael, Mary Bedford, Ms. Herford and Susan Taylor there was always much more to education. Painting, clay, balsa wood and basket weaving all came into it somewhere. Moreover, like all loyal members of the Nature Study Group, I adored Miss Taylor, a young woman who forthrightly resisted the strange injunction for boys to address their female teachers as 'sir'. On a good day, her lessons would be interrupted by the need to inspect unusual birds caught for ringing in the school mist net. She remains the

*Hugh Lindeman at Bateman Street in 1950*

only teacher I have ever known to impersonate a short-sighted elephant while being 'stalked' by her pupils. When Stanley Stubbs told the senior school of her untimely death in a car crash in Sweden in 1966 many of the boys who knew her burst spontaneously into tears.

The Prep in the early Sixties can be celebrated for its pedagogic excellence, but also for its mildly eccentric team sports where Foresters could be defeated at cricket by the Corinthians, and Barbarians never played rugby. My own view of its qualities was coloured by a fourth year of junior schooling spent not in Cambridge, but in Khartoum where my father took sabbatical leave. For two terms, my education passed from empathy and encouragement to the scorpions (metaphorical) and whips (real enough) of Italian Catholic priests. Other aspects of life in the Sudan were treasurable, but after six months I certainly knew what I was missing back in Trumpington Road.

For my first two terms at the upper school, I became a less-than-delighted junior boarder. Bedtimes were earlier than I was used to, and a whole hobbies room consecrated to Airfix modelling did not compensate. When angry, Commander Keith Symons, as both house and form master, sometimes resorted to corporal punishment in a way that detracted from his more habitual cheer. He was also my introduction to that odd tendency for boys to refer to staff by plausible first names that happened to be wrong. Although Cecil Crouch in the Art Room was allowed to be 'Cess', Keith Symons was somehow 'Ken', David Dunkley became 'Dennis' and John Tanfield was, eternally, 'Charlie T'. Genuine nicknames such as David 'Spider' Webber and Victor 'Seedy' Sederman made more obvious sense, although not necessarily to their owners. 'Kink' was surely not applied to Keith Barry before the Sixties when some bright spark made a lateral association between his more conventional nickname 'KB' and the then-fashionable 'kinky boots'. As a Sixth Former, however, I was astonished to be asked by Hugh Percival, a family friend, why the boys called him 'Bucket'. Thankfully, the answer - derived from his preferred term for a wastepaper bin - was not too embarrassing to explain. That Stanley Stubbs was never more than 'Stan', may have reflected his imposing and somewhat remote, presence. His upbraiding of the school following reports from the Eastern Counties Bus Company of anti-social behaviour on the 106 ("to think that any of my boys...!") was impressive, but fortunately also quite imitable. On the few occasions I spoke to him, he was encouraging and benign. Yet, I remained as much in awe of him in 1969 when he retired as I had been five years earlier when I shook with nerves in the post-assembly 'late' queue.

My impression of the teaching staff is affected by an early bias towards arts subjects. Scientists would contribute a more coherent view of David Webber, for example, than a look of undisguised surprise after I scraped

*Susan Taylor*

through 'O' level physics. Mathematicians would have better memories of Bob Whittaker, than his decidedly 'Weary' response to cricketing failures by the Colts. 'Jack' Gerish never taught me chemistry, yet he loomed large for several rugby seasons as I attained occasional membership of the First XV. Sport always seemed important in the Stubbs era. Routine defeats by such tough and distant teams as Gresham's in Norfolk did not seem to matter, so long as we could see off local competition from Cambridgeshire High School for Boys and The Leys. Unfortunately, in my Sixth Form years even that was often beyond us. The only conspicuously successful team I ever played for was the Third Hockey XI. I was, however, an enthusiastic participant in games of hand tennis, played during break times across a line of brief cases, on the concrete base of a demolished hut near the geography room.

*Douglas Brown*
*by John Garbutt*
*The drawing appeared on*
*the programme cover of the*
**Festival of the Mummery**
*1965*

Back indoors, the Mummery captured my imagination from the outset. Even the termly 'speeches' that terrified many of my peers were a source of pleasure. Chris Parry was in strict, but creative charge. The influence of the late Douglas Brown was felt from the commemorative Festival of the Mummery, which replaced the school play in my first year, to the reverence with which David Roulinson, seven years later, described a lesson that Brown constructed around a single line from Othello. We were, meanwhile, fortunate, to become the first group of third years to make use of the Senior Mummery created in the former Scout Hut. Keith Crook's less formal style of teaching was taken as gratifying (and mostly undeserved) recognition of increasing maturity. His advocacy of film as well as 20th century drama and poetry shifted our literary centre of gravity forward by at least a couple of centuries.

Three years of boarding between the Fourth and Lower Sixth years, meant the two English teachers that I came to know best were Keith Barry, the Senior Housemaster and Alastair Langlands, the Tutor, who had by now taken over the (Junior) Mummery. Although there was a certain formality about Keith and his wife Beryl, there were also depths of kindness and understanding for which I will always be grateful. As parents should, Keith set boundaries. But he was also prepared to move with the times, especially if a good case (key word: 'reasonable') could be made for doing so. One result was that we became the first boarders to attend the Girls' High School dance and to take part in unsupervised play rehearsals with Perse girls. Although their teaching styles were quite different, Keith and Alastair communicated a love of literature. Alastair, whose flair extended to a monocle, three-piece suits and a veteran Bentley, had such a well-developed sense of humour that he would nowadays be suspected of post-modern irony. His productions of house and school plays were uproarious for the performers, and quite possibly for the audience as well.

No recollection of staff 'characters' could omit John Tanfield. Who else could begin an A-level lesson at precisely the point in the reign of James I that he previously left off, yet – on being reminded that this was supposed to be a European history period – switch effortlessly to another monologue on the Thirty Years War. By 1970, however, certain world-weariness was evident: not least in his choice of productions of the school play. Few can quote the opening lines of Ford's obscure Perkin Warbeck, and I suspect that most of them are former Perse Players. Malcolm McFarlane, ruler of the wave tank in the Geography Room, was another outstanding teacher with the knack of bringing his subject to life, as was Tony Billinghurst who inadvertently turned the Place d'Italie, Paris into a place of pilgrimage. Sadly, those filmstrip aids to elementary French, la famille Thibaud ("Répétez la classe: 'Monsieur Thibaud est ingénieur'") were not home the day I called. Approaching retirement, Hugh Percival remained a lively classroom presence and motivator, although selective use of a hearing aid that subsequently stood him in good stead as a local politician was sometimes in evidence. Among the relative newcomers, David Weigall stood out as a stimulating history teacher and Graham Sudbury coaxed school music into crackling life from a very low ebb.

*John Tanfield*
*in 1969*

As a First former, I witnessed one of the last impromptu, end-of-year cap-burning rituals in the car park by members of the Fifth form. I nevertheless, associate real change in the life of the school with the arrival of Tony Melville. This is partly personal, because I do not think it likely that Stanley Stubbs would have appointed anyone who was not a member of the CCF as Head of School. But Tony's willingness to adjust and improve on tradition was manifest in areas as varied as the introduction of a School Council, permission for a rock concert in the school hall, creation of a tuck shop in the pavilion and the (almost) democratic arrangements for managing the new Sixth Form Centre. Not everyone liked the changes Tony instituted or appreciated his offbeat sense of humour. His determination to apply disciplinary sanctions when his wider boundaries were crossed brought him enemies as well as friends. The discovery that the cast of the first-ever Lower Sixth play had been smoking in the Senior Mummery produced a stern reprimand, but the show went on. But he and Keith Barry felt bound to respond with temporary suspension from school for members of the senior dormitory who shinned down a drainpipe on the last weekend of the summer term 1970, for a night on the town. There was consternation at the time, but no enduring consequences for most of those involved (my own dilemma was hypothetical since I was away on exeat). Later that year, however, when one of those who had been suspended sent a picture to the *Cambridge Evening News* of a lone sardine that was unfairly alleged to be the extent of a boarding house tea, the immutable result was expulsion.

Challenges to authority, thereafter, did seem to multiply. Drugs, which for most of my school career had meant nothing more sinister than sulphonamide powder pumped down the throats of boys with tonsillitis, began to surface as an issue. More traditional problems, such as bullying or truancy were, so far as I could tell, rare. My guess is that school life was generally too interesting and the staff and pupils too motivated for either to become institutionalised. The routine conflicts of those days were over such sartorial matters as hair length (progressively longer), the definition of a 'blue' shirt and the admissibility of elastic-sided suede boots. Rock music and the exchange of LPs were endemic. Interest in sex was no less strong, but largely theoretical. One of Tony Melville's innovations in this respect was an afternoon in the lecture theatre for Lower Sixth boys where a doctor and nurse discussed human reproduction in more accurate terms. The session was chiefly remarkable for being the only lesson in my entire school career when tea and biscuits were served.

Readers may have noticed that the limited evidence I have produced of a school influenced by 'Sixties' liberation and rebellion is almost entirely derived from events in the early Seventies. This might be taken as proof of that other much-repeated proposition that "if you remember the Sixties you weren't really there." Except that I do remember my eleven years of education at the Perse very well and with enduring affection. Forty years on, they still seem far from revolting.

**THE PERSE IN THE 1960s**

*By ANDREW REICHER*

I joined the school in the last year of the Prep, in September 1964, after my parents had come to Cambridge from the West Country earlier that year. I moved to the senior school in 1965. At the end of 1966, my father accepted a job in Geneva. My mother remained in Cambridge until the end of the 1966/67 school year and then moved to Switzerland. I therefore became a boarder in September 1967 and entered the Senior House where I remained until leaving the school in December 1972 after taking my Cambridge Scholarship exams.

The experience of boarders in a school where about 90% of the students live at home, is of course unrepresentative. Many of my memories are of boarding, rather than of school life. At the time, the "swinging sixties", it seemed terribly restrictive and that we were missing all the fun. But in retrospect, it was a very safe and happy experience with just one or two shifts of danger. The figure of most immediate authority was that of Keith Barry, the Housemaster. Keith seemed to me at the age of 13 an old, strict and unrelenting disciplinarian with a limited sense of humour. By the time he left the house in 1972 to be replaced by David

Dunkley, I realised there was a lot more to him than that, including a dry, but very acute sense of humour. In fact, if you are a Housemaster looking after 30+ adolescent boys without seeing the funny side, I think you will probably end up insane.

We all believed that Keith was so unobservant that, through great cunning and careful concealment, most of our defiant breaches of rules were completely unremarked. He can't have known what we were up to because, had he the slightest inkling of what we were doing, this martinet would have visited the most awful retribution on any apprehended offender. It began to dawn on me that this might not be the case early in the Lower Sixth. Returning from a legitimate evening outing at which most of us had imbibed a number of (obviously illicit) drinks, we encountered Keith at the foot of the stairs and had to make our way past him. One of our number, Richard Morgan, was very much the worse for wear, and Keith engaged him in jolly conversation for several minutes – on Richard's part almost totally incoherent – before allowing him to escape to the sanctuary of the dormitory. Richard was later asked, "do you think he noticed anything?", and replied "no, not a thing!". It would have taken a blind, deaf man with no sense of smell whatsoever to reach such a conclusion, and after this I increasingly realised that Keith noticed precisely what he chose to.

*Keith and Beryl Barry on the occasion of their Golden Wedding Anniversary*

In the Sixth Form, I came to know him and his wife, Beryl, as warm, caring, civilised, humorous, but intensely sensible and morally tough people. Never petty, Keith turned a blind eye to trivial indiscretions, but put his foot down when he had to. Not in the least trendy, he moved with the times at an appropriate speed and gave all of us in his care a set of fixed reference points with which to make our way through a turbulent outside world. I owe an enormous personal debt of gratitude to Keith and Beryl for their stint in loco parentis. I hope Keith and Beryl and others remembered here will forgive me for some of these recollections, which are written in a spirit of what I actually remember (which may be coloured by imagination) and total affection.

Other memories of boarding, in no particular order, and certainly not chronologically, include:

Matron. Sybil Grey. A plump, smiling, kind and then middle-aged lady with a no-nonsense approach to central heating in dormitories and illness among boys. Bedsocks were the answer. To my recollection, I never had a day off sick during the whole of my time at the Boarding House. In those days, we got clean underwear once a week, distributed by Matron, which hardly seems believable now.

*[Budget constraints on Housemasters were indeed tight. Ed.]*

House Food. Quite poor, and sometimes inadequate, I believe constrained by tight budgets imposed to keep boarding fees affordable. After a particularly lean spell, we got a single sardine on a dinner plate for tea (admittedly with toast and margarine available from the side table in the dining room). The plates were large and prominently carried the school crest. One boy, a keen photographer but in trouble for various reasons, took a picture of one of the plates with its single fish in the middle and sent it to the *Cambridge Evening News*, who published it on the letters page. We thought this great fun, but Tony Melville and Keith and Beryl were genuinely scandalised and upset, and the culprit, after owning up, was expelled. I really can't remember if the quantities of food increased after this episode.

An institution which did spring up was the collection by bicycle of takeaway food from fast food outlets on Chesterton Road by junior boys, whose "tip" was a free portion for themselves. The most popular variety was Chinese. David Tang was an enthusiastic patron of this arrangement. Recently, I was lucky enough to visit the China Club in Hong Kong at David's invitation. I'm glad to report that the food bore absolutely no relation whatsoever to our previous shared Chinese dinners.

Showers after Rugby, and sitting on the enormous old-fashioned radiators in the Prep room and studies, eating toast, to warm up on cold days.

Getting into big trouble in the Fifth Form. This was the 69/70 school year. A number of older boys began going out to town by climbing out of the dormitory windows after lights out, leaving a cunning and totally convincing "dummy" of clothing in their beds and returning in the small hours of the morning. I believe one of them actually kept an ancient motor cycle for this purpose in the bushes at the bottom of the boarding house grounds. Their meeting point with their acquaintances was reportedly a kebab restaurant in Rose Crescent, after which they were said to attend a sequence of glamorous and swinging parties with the day boys and university students. More and more people began to accompany them. Towards the end of term, a particularly large gathering was planned. Being a coward, I wanted to go along and see what all the fuss was about but was afraid of the consequences of being caught. It was clear from the conversations that those who didn't go that night would be regarded as both wet and yellow. I think practically the whole senior dormitory slipped down the drainpipe and made their way to Rose Crescent, and who-knew-what debauched and exciting event afterwards. I decided to participate.

Well, the kebab house was really very boring, and the people who knew where the action was weren't there. So at about midnight, I set off back to the boarding house alone, fed up that what had been billed as a night of excitement was turning out very tedious. On the way back, I was set upon by a group of youths who jumped out of a car on Trumpington Road and roughed me up. So I was rather dejected on my way back to Glebe Road. But my dejection was nothing to the state into which I was sent by the news on climbing back into the dormitory that we had all been caught. We were all suspended until the end of the term and in deep disgrace. I learned a number of lessons from this. For example, don't always believe schoolboys' stories. Don't feel you have to do things you don't want to simply to earn the approbation of your peers. And so on. But on balance and 30 years later, I would rather have had this experience than stayed in the dormitory and wished I'd had the courage to be naughty. And the memory of it has certainly also helped me in bringing up my own children.

Alastair Langlands. The house tutor for my first two years at the boarding house, used to read the junior dormitory bedtime stories in instalments. I particularly remember Evelyn Waugh's "Decline and Fall". It was brilliant, and I subsequently read most of Waugh's work, comic and serious. Mr Langlands owned an ancient Bentley, which often would not start unassisted. His punishment system was to put miscreants on a list for later early-morning push starting duties. I'm sure there must be residents of Glebe Road at the time who remember this large, dilapidated vehicle, majestically rolling out of the drive and lumbering down the road, pushed by a motley collection of five or six scruffy adolescent boys, before the engine wheezed into life and it sailed off in a cloud of exhaust fumes. Alastair possessed a wardrobe of rather elegant tweedy tailored suits. He had a slightly affected old-fashioned mien, but we all liked him and were sorry to see him leave to be Head, I believe, of a middle school in Suffolk. He must now be in his early sixties.

*Alastair Langlands*

David Tang's driving lessons. Alastair Langlands' Bentley leads naturally to David Tang's Rolls Royce. David shared a study with me and is one of the most naturally good-humoured people I've ever known. He never seemed to get dejected and always saw the funny side of every situation, which he expressed with gales of laughter. We knew his family was reasonably well-to-do. When he turned 17, his father sent their London chauffeur to Cambridge to give David driving lessons at weekends. The magnificent latest model Rolls Royce would appear. "L" plates would be attached, and off David would go for his practice sessions. The rest of us were highly impressed by this phenomenon.

Companionship. I remember long conversations in studies and dormitories, both serious and frivolous. Playing billiards on a shabby table in the common room. I remember listening to the Beatles' White Album after lights out on a transistor radio in the dormitory (John Grace again) on Radio Caroline. I remember laughing a lot. I also remember long, tedious, wet Sunday afternoons. We were also pretty horrible sometimes to some of the boarders who didn't conform to notions of "cool". But on the whole, it was a happy, safe and reasonably civilised existence.

So much for boarding. What of school life? Let me give you some snapshots in similar format.

Scout Camp. I know I went to West Runton in the summer of 1966 at the end of my first year in the senior school, because I can vividly remember listening to the World Cup Final on a transistor radio as England won. I can still see in my mind's eye the aerial runway from a tree in the corner of the site, running across the latrine pit towards firm ground. All the little ones were terrified of indefinite suspension above the pit until we had no option but to fall into it! There were also exciting late night wide games and camp fires.

Theatre. The Mummery system and other experiences have inspired in me a lifetime's passion for the theatre. School plays were wonderful experiences, especially directed by John Tanfield (see below). I was an execrably bad actor but like to think that I could have made a somewhat better director, especially after a Lower Sixth production of "She Stoops to Conquer" in the senior Mummery hut which we put on ourselves with actresses from the High School for Girls on Long Road. It was clear, however, that the game was up when Bill Buffery began starring in most of the shows.

In 1970 we were taken to Stratford-upon-Avon to see Peter Brook's famous and enormously influential production of "A Midsummer Night's Dream". I will never forget the excitement, joy and passion of that evening. The set, if I remember correctly, was a scaffolding framework, from which swings were hung and on which much of the action took place. The energy and pace of the production were spellbinding. It was very slick and everything worked very precisely. But through it all shone the poetry and beauty of the language and one wondered how a provincial Englishman over 400 years ago could have imagined such stuff. Never after that could any English literature lessons be all dull.

Games. I am a very indifferent but enthusiastic player of ball games. Rugby, as played in those days, suited me fine, because one could cover up a lack of technical skill with enthusiasm and effort. My year group was relatively weak and in our first two years of representing the School found ourselves on the end of fearful beatings, until we came to the Colts. Our coach for that year was John Gerrish, the Welsh Chemistry teacher. He was an inspiration and turned a very ordinary group of boys

*The Prefects 1964*

into a competitive unit by instilling into us a belief in ourselves and fierce determination to win, which up till then had been lacking. We started to train with real gusto and to win games. The highlight of my entire school sports career was the Colts rugby game against The Leys. In the previous two years they had beaten us by cricket scores. This time again, they put us under pressure from the start. Robert Pearson, our year's star, a natural ball player and very tough, intercepted a Leys pass inside our "25" (we used to measure pitches in yards) and ran the entire length of the field to score a try in the first 15 minutes. 3-0 to us (in those days a try was only worth 3 points). My memory tells me that we withstood heavy pressure from The Leys for the whole of the rest of the game, with them camped inside our "25" for most of the time, and never came close to scoring ourselves, to win by that score. Our year never again beat The Leys at rugby. That episode impressed very strongly upon me the importance of motivation, and the possibilities for willpower and determination to achieve unlikely results, both in sport and in other aspects of life.

Geography. I am one of the generation of boys who went on trips to the Peak District led by Malcolm McFarlane. Malcolm was another larger-than-life character who defined the School in the 1960s and 70s. School exam papers were produced on a duplicating machine which reproduced text hand-written with a stylus on a wax-coated sheet of paper. Malcolm's handwriting was rather spidery. In our O level mock paper, which was one of the last we sat, one question read something along the lines of "explain why most mining in Ghana takes place near the coast". My friend Lawrence West-Knights, for whom Geography was not a favourite subject, had done very limited revision, getting up at 6.00am that morning to try to cram in as much as possible before the exam from his rather meagre set of notes. But when the time came there were very few questions on the paper he felt able to answer. There was a splodge on the duplicating sheet over the "m" of "most mining", and, in his tiredness, Lawrence read this as a "k" rather than an "m". So the question appeared to him to read "explain why kost mining takes place near the coast…" Kost? Lawrence decided this must be some very useful mineral we had been told about in a lesson to which he had paid minimal attention. So he made up an answer to the question explaining the economic importance of "kost" to the Ghanaian economy, with maps showing the location of the kost deposits and the railway lines to get it to the ports.

Malcolm had a very stentorian voice. When he returned our mock papers to us, there was a long pause after Lawrence was given his. Malcolm fixed him with a glare, and at the top of his voice, in a tone of withering contempt, shouted "kost, laddie….kost!!!" A glorious and priceless memory.

*The Perse CCF glider, now in the Shuttleworth Collection*

The CCF. I joined the RAF section. Experiences this opened included glider courses at RAF airfields in old winch-launched open cockpit two-seater aircraft, sailing under the auspices of the Royal Navy section in Norfolk Broads sailing cruisers (trying to evade the boats with the masters on them so we could visit the waterside pubs) and, best of all, a flying scholarship.

To get this, I had to attend the Officer and Aircrew Selection Centre at RAF Biggin Hill, which was a very exciting experience in its own right. On winning the award, I requested to attend a flying school in the South. Because of this, or for some other reason, they sent me to the Channel Islands Aero Club flying school on the island of Jersey. So for almost the entire summer holiday between the first and second years of the Sixth Form, I stayed in a Bed & Breakfast in St. Brelades Bay and turned up every day at the airport to learn to fly. Cross-country exercises involved flying to St. Malo, Rennes and Granville, sometimes on my own, and being directed around the skies above the island by Air Traffic Control in a single-engine Cessna in the company of jets from Gatwick and Luton! And this was all when I was 17. I got my private pilot's licence before my driver's licence.

History. I save the best till last. History was my favourite subject. The teaching was wonderful. John Tanfield and David Weigall made the subject come alive. The Tudor Reformation, Cardinal Wolsey, Thomas Cromwell, Star Chamber. And then the seventeenth century and the English Civil War. Europe and the wars of religion. Followed by the 18th century, the Enlightenment, British mercantilism and the growth of Empire in India and North America. The War of American Independence, the French Revolution, the Napoleonic wars and the Industrial Revolution. In the A level course, we got into 19th century British and European history, especially the unification of Germany and Italy.

*Hugh Percival*

The two of them were great characters and excellent teachers. They stimulated one to imagine what life was like in the relevant period and the reasons the protagonists in all the great events we covered did what they did. It wasn't a dry recital of events and dates, but came alive. In many ways, it was similar to theatre and drama. I loved it, and read voraciously. Those of us interested in the subject weren't treated like children, but were shown how to explore the subject. They asked thought-provoking questions and guided us towards correct areas of enquiry.

I genuinely feel that John Tanfield and David Weigall each enjoyed debating the subject with their students, even though we were clearly naïve and inexperienced and they had gone over the subjects umpteen times before. They were both quite inspirational teachers.

As I continue to write, I warm to the task. Much comes flooding back. I'd like to do justice to all the dedicated and decent people who taught me, and who I haven't mentioned so far. People like Hugh Percival (Latin), Bob Whittaker (Maths), David Webber (Physics), and many, many others.

I remember a safe, comfortable, probably a little unsophisticated environment, but one in which I felt generally very happy. I don't recall any real aggression or unpleasantness. It was a community of transparent decency. So it has been a real pleasure to try to call back these experiences.

### THE PERSE IN THE 1970s

*By ANDREW SUMNALL, Head of the School 1979-1980*

It's a brave decision asking a doctor to write an article – are Bletchley Park deciphering skills still available in Cambridge? So, if your name is mis-spelt later on … don't blame the printers!

I'd been well briefed about the 'small fish, big pool' syndrome of going up to the Upper School. No one had mentioned the dangers of being crushed to death on the stairs at first break. The stampede to the tuck shop seemed a more justifiable risk: 'no pain, no gain' translated to 'no Chelsea bun' if you weren't quick, an early lesson in Darwinian evolution. Doughnuts and chocolate were a big improvement on the cold milk we'd had at break at the Prep.

Most of my 'year of 72' had come up together from the Prep; I recognised one or two others from previous encounters. One (now) friend had sidelined me in a football match against his primary school the previous year. I can still feel the lump on my shin now, Kearia. Many of the boys in the three years ahead I also knew. Prefects however were an unknown quantity. What did they actually do? We watched the third and fourth years test them out: Reicher, the Head Boy, seemed very stern. By contrast, Charlie Kidman, his deputy, seemed to spend all his time laughing or smiling. I can't recall much about the schoolwork at all from my early years. I remember being very surprised we were going to spend all our English lessons as two competing theatre companies, with the pros of not doing any formal grammar. The con of having to sit at the front soon outweighed this, as did trying to organise my fifteen players. Did Paul Bogan take over from me? He now has a career in theatre management… My greatest love at school was always the sport, but even there the first six months brought a lot of change. As one of the smallest boys in the school (in fact, the fourth; I can name the other three), rugby was a nightmare. At least getting run over (by Nick Hindmarsh, Richard Sills *et alia*) kept you warm though. In the Lent term, if you actually got onto a pitch (rain or snow usually got there first), then the danger was being so frozen you couldn't get off again at the end. I remember crying in the changing room after one game because my hands were so frozen I couldn't get my boots off.

The last practice of the term the sun did shine at last, tempers frayed, some professional fouls led to my friend John pursuing my co-conspirator Nick around the pitch, hotly followed by Mr Pogson. Mr Pogson won; was this the original use of the sin-bin in English sport?

(John also provided my most enjoyable moment in Rugby. Having spent two seasons 1) never making a tackle and 2) not getting muddy, he was rumbled by David Baker. The game was stopped – a suitably boggy patch was located and John made to fall on the ball, followed by the rest of the scrum, 'Chunky' Chalmers and 'Ganger' Wolfenden and all. I suspect this sort of thing is now outlawed by European legislation, but it enriched the lives of the other twenty-nine players, and no doubt DB too.)

The change to summer weather was always welcome: I only remember fast hard cricket wickets and bright sunshine. I don't know how easy the grounds were to look after in those days, but the playing area was much more extensive than now, as the buildings had encroached less; but certainly Mr Wagstaff and then Doug Collard produced pitches as good as anywhere else we played.

Was there cultural life at the Perse in the early 70s too? I remember two Perse Players' productions: *Coriolanus*, with Bill Buffery as the lead; and the *Pirates of Penzance*, with Ray Revell as the Major General. It was a big success. But it was also controversial; partly as a lot of Masters took part, and were alleged to have 'nicked' parts from the older boys; partly as the Masters turned out to be

*Mr Wagstaff*

rather good at it; and partly because Dr Parry produced it, and he was controversial anyway. I think we were a bit young to understand why this was, but suspected it had something to do with the leather trousers and riding a motorbike.

Do Geography field trips count as culture? Dottrell (or was it Doggerel) Hall Farm was memorable for mud and getting lost, and the litany of crop rotations: 'set-aside' doesn't scan as well as 'break'. Derbyshire was on a different scale – a different scale of lostness and muddiness. The coach journey seemed endless. The number of medieval field systems we passed was endless. Once there though, it became more of a holiday, the only time in seven years the whole seventy of us were away together. I don't remember the trip home. I think we all slept…

Work did intervene in a major fashion at 'O' level. The scope of what we had to cover was daunting, but I expect it's much worse now. We had a groundbreaking English Language 'O' level continuously assessed by Dr Parry. It included drama (mostly 'Pete and Dud' sketches), and a talk each. Pete Winckles did one on the Mersey Tunnel. I think mine was on prehistoric sheep. If only camcorders had existed then!

English Literature 'O' level the following year proved eventful too. Keith Barry hadn't taught our year before this, and we were apprehensive he'd be stern, and it'd be dull. Anything but, once we'd caught onto his dry sense of humour: "that's the rub, as it were!" Sam Buttery proved inspired reading *Henry V* in his American accent, if hard to stop mid-flow. And Thomas Hardy spawned the rock operetta 'Far from the Madding Crowd' which premiered after the exams. "I've got the sheep blast high" and "Bathsheba, just like a young farmer should" were sensational. Quinty (no need for a surname here) and the bananas were also sensational, tho' I did feel sorry for Pete Hutt the caretaker afterwards. I think we did try to clear up.

End of 'O' levels meant the Lower Sixth; and Lower Sixth gave the opportunity to play first team sport. The Saggers/Graves/Long/Stovin/Pearson eras were passed; it was our year's chance. The first term, the Rugby wasn't a success. How 'Doc' Powell endured defeat after defeat I don't know, (64-3 against Gresham's at Holt was a School record at the time), but somehow he managed to find something positive each time to take forward to the next game.

Hockey and Cricket proved much happier hunting grounds over the next two years. I wish we'd had the chance to play hockey on all-weather surfaces like later generations. We had two outstanding players. Robert Fowlds' weight of shot and timing brought a first-half hat trick against Bishop's Stortford, sweet revenge for David Dunkley after the injustice of the previous year's defeat (with a better side than ours). And John Wilkinson won county caps while still at School, a feat the rest of us didn't appreciate fully at the time.

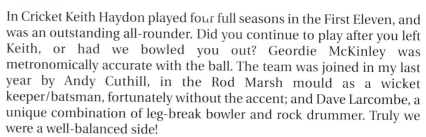

*David (Doc) Powell*

In Cricket Keith Haydon played four full seasons in the First Eleven, and was an outstanding all-rounder. Did you continue to play after you left Keith, or had we bowled you out? Geordie McKinley was metronomically accurate with the ball. The team was joined in my last year by Andy Cuthill, in the Rod Marsh mould as a wicket keeper/batsman, fortunately without the accent; and Dave Larcombe, a unique combination of leg-break bowler and rock drummer. Truly we were a well-balanced side!

'A' levels caused a lot of anxiety, understandably so in terms of the high stakes and expectations. In reality though, in the sciences the standard of teaching was so high that the exams were as 'low risk' for a catastrophe as these things can ever be. I imagine in the arts the questions were much less predictable. The other distractions, the Scouts and the CCF and the sport avoided the claustrophobia and intensity that I later found with exams at university. And we had some great parties when the exams ended.

My seventh and last term was very low key by comparison. As Head Boy I'd had two nightmares; slipping on the tiger skin in Tony Melville's study and my speech on Speech Day. I thought I'd escaped when two days before I got a black eye in Rugby against King's School, Ely. But unfortunately I was passed fit for the day; fortunately my mum and dad wrote most of the speech, and it passed off OK.

There's so much I haven't included here; the great times we had on CCF camps or expeditions for example. I realise this is a very personal reminiscence and the memories of my contemporaries in the 1970s will be very different. My apologies not to include more of those in the years that followed us. Now, with my hopes for the education of my sons, I realise how lucky I was; I hope they will be as fortunate. And I hope the Perse, Prep and Senior schools, continue to flourish.

## THE PERSE IN THE 1980s

*by MATTHEW JORDAN OP 1979-1990*

The pupils of the 1970s probably did not fully comprehend the quirkiness and eccentricity of the Perse in that decade, but the 1980s included its gradual evolution into a far more mainstream independent school, and as I began my reflection on the school in the '80s, the most notable impression was the gradual erosion of those peculiarities.

The Perse began the 1980s a small school with low fees, focused singularly on academics, with a slightly anarchic, cynical, anti-establishment culture. No doubt the most significant moment of the 1970s for the school was the abolition of the Direct Grant system and the school's transition to fully independent status; but I think it was the mid-80s that saw the consequent culture change.

In January 1980 the school had around 415 pupils; there were just two forms per year, 'A' and 'Alpha'. But the loss of Direct Grant status left the school fending for itself financially. Simultaneously it faced real competition for the first time, from Hills Road Sixth Form College. The

*The Prefects of 1990, Matthew Jordan seated far right*

school's answer to these two issues was to increase fee income by increasing the number of pupils, but also to improve its offer by reducing class sizes, with the adoption of a third form per year-group.

To my mind it was this expansion in the number of pupils that led to the gradual dilution of the school's somewhat eccentric culture. The number of pupils grew by over 20% through the mid-1980s and the fees rose significantly. As a consequence the school necessarily reduced the academic requirements for entry; its teaching methods and the subjects it offered became more progressive; and yet its outlook and culture became more establishment and conservative, reflecting the change in its constituency.

Whereas arguments raged in the early 1980s about whether a smoking hut should be built for the Sixth form, I cannot imagine that my own year-group would have entered this discussion; we knew the outcome without having the debate. The irreverent School Revues and the underground magazines of the early 1980s had fizzled out by Dr Stephen's era. Even *The Pelican* had carried anti-establishment, anti-staff, anti-school-policy articles and letters in the early 1980s; by the end of the decade it was increasingly the mouthpiece of the school. A baboon could have stood as the Conservative candidate in the school's mock election in 1987, and it would have won. In fact, that is more or less what did happen. The cane was abandoned on Dr Stephen's arrival. And, in 1989, the greatest of all school institutions became extinct: Chelsea buns disappeared from the tuck shop when the local baker closed down.

An attempt to distil the impressions of several years into a few lines inevitably exaggerates the views conveyed. I have implied above that the school was as free-spirited as Summerhill in 1980 and as conservative as the Women's Institute by 1990. In truth, this culture change was gradual, evolutionary, and natural: there did not appear to be any suppression from on high. The change also had benefits: as the school's cynical, anti-establishment culture was eroded, a more self-confident, egotistic nature emerged, and this was much needed. I well remember Alistair King's letter to *The Pelican* in the mid-1980s deriding the school for its lack of self-belief. He made a valid point: the school's cynicism was in many ways its undoing. The pupils just didn't believe in the place. They didn't see the Perse as one of the best academic schools in the country, which it was; they saw it as an also-ran, a has-been harking back to a ghost-like patriarch called Dr Rouse. That the school ended the '80s more self-confident and self-believing must be a good thing.

In these years, Tony Melville led the transformation of the school's facilities. By 1980 the original 1961 buildings were almost unchanged. The school had just one music room, no seminar rooms, no theatre, no sports hall, no all-weather surface, and the school did not own a computer. The masters' Common Room was then just one small room

*'... the constant drone of cement mixers.'*

near the administration block. Where the masters' Common Room now stands was the croquet lawn; and half the school was taught English in a wooden hut at the far end of the parade ground. the Perse was a truly small place. This too changed as pupil numbers increased, and scarcely a year went by without the constant drone of cement mixers. By the end of the decade the facilities had been dramatically improved.

But if the 1980s were a decade of change, the biggest change was the arrival of a new headmaster; the appointment of Martin Stephen in 1987 as Headmaster was a watershed. He imprinted on the pupils an element of his own character – self-belief, modernisation, ambition. As a pupil, the culture change was immediate and noticeable. He reinforced this by reinforcing the school's infrastructure: pastoral care, tutors, and an array of new managerial roles (Head of Sixth Form, Director of Studies, Emperor of the Stationery Cupboard, you name it).

*An elegant Graham Sudbury supervising games. Cartoon by Simon Wells*

A school's atmosphere is defined primarily by its staff, and the staff was full of characters in the 1980s – probably just as much as in the 1970s. Mr Sudbury was awarded the accolade 'Most Elegant Man in Cambridge' by the *Cambridge Evening News*. Sounds of *Radio Ga-Ga* by Queen and *Happy Talk* by Captain Sensible emanated from Mr Wearing's Art Room. An inveterate door-slammer, the only time Mr Wearing lost his sense of humour was when one first year pupil stuck an eraser to the door frame, causing it to catapult back into the room upon his habitual slam.

Mr Billinghurst's collection of Rover cars was so ancient that one almost expected to see Harold Macmillan climbing out of them. Mr Nierinck used the command 'I want to hear a pin drop' on boys as old as 16. I remember copying Gary Milner-Moore's Geography homework word-for-word in 1987; Mr McFarlane gave Gary an 'A' and me a 'B+'. Travesty? My brother was once in the back of Mr McFarlane's car in the car in the early '80s as he swerved in and out of traffic en route to a CCF fixture. Finally tiring of being hooted he wound down the window and yelled to the passing drivers 'Can't you see I'm trying to eat a bag of chips?'

The Geography department experienced a major change in 1985 when Malcolm McFarlane went into semi-retirement to be replaced by Richard Crabtree with his omnipresent coffee mug and his omnipotent

*Richard Crabtree in the pillory at the annual fund-raising Scout Fair*

*Malcolm McFarlane, in retirement still supporting the School, opening the new astroturf pitch in 1995*

Scout Troop. I am certain that the Scout Troop, at its height under Richard's leadership in the mid-1980s, must have been one of the very best in the country. Richard deserves a medal for the sheer effort he put into the Troop in the '80s. It was, as Dr Stephen described it, one of the jewels in the school's crown.

The Maths department seemed to be cursed in the 1980s. Mr Whittaker had to come out of retirement twice: once when Mr Pinhey was seriously ill, and also upon Mr Hepworth's untimely death. Mr Whittaker's decision to teach Maths to the first year in my year was an unwise experiment with mind-expanding education. He seemed to want to prove to himself that first formers really could be cajoled into understanding calculus given the right level of prodding. Panic and tense parents' evenings ensued, along with many memorable occasions when Mr Whittaker fell off the platform at the front of the room whilst engrossed in indecipherable squiggles on the blackboard, crying 'Dammit, I must get that fixed!' as he collided with the waste bin. Even these scenes hardly compare with another teacher's utter inability to keep control of his lessons, once declaring to the class 'I'm going to stop teaching you, you're all being so horrible to me' and sitting in chalky misery whilst the class continued to enact a scene from the terraces at Millwall.

The English department was equally filled with characters. The mummery system was still flourishing under Mr Roulinson, whose excellent teaching was occasionally overshadowed by his fearsome nature. I remember on my second day at the school addressing him as 'Mr Roulinson'. He cut my question off with the stony response 'It is customary to address masters as "sir" in this school'. The difference with the Prep School, where Miss Bedford might have called one a 'silly cuckoo', was stark!

One teacher in the mid-80s, did his best to make Liberace look butch, and few will forget Mr Porter making latecomers to his classes 'go and stand in the bin'. Tony Porter contributed enormously to school life in the 1980s, primarily with his direction of the Perse Players. Although often criticised for his dictatorial style as a director, his results were consistently excellent, from *A Voyage Round my father*, *Inherit the Wind* and *Macbeth* in the early 80s to *Forty Years On* and *Amadeus* at the end of the decade.

On the field the school was regularly embarrassed, being beaten at almost every sport by the otherwise poor-relation of Cambridge schooling, The Leys. The one benefit of this was Mr Vodden's candour about the atrocity of his teams in his sporting reviews that seemed to double the length of every *Pelican* in the second half of the decade.

Despite Mr Tanfield's retirement in the early 1980s the History Department flourished, thanks to the combination of Mr Roberts' single-minded devotion to Oliver Cromwell and Mr Jones' enactment of various historical episodes, highlights of which included end-of-term medieval feasts and a demonstration of Henry II's epileptic fits complete with DJ laughing hysterically, standing on his desk and biting his chair.

Few would disagree with me for claiming that Dr McKechnie wins the title 'Character of the 80s'. He arrived as a student teacher in the Classics Department under Mr Shannon in a sky-blue Robin Reliant three-wheeler, built around 1970. Although he once proclaimed to an amused audience that 'on a good day with a fair wind behind me I've seen the speedometer reach 80mph', boys would linger behind after school just to have the pleasure of overtaking Dr McKechnie on their bikes as he drove down the avenue towards Hills Road. Upon his appointment to the school, in an effort to convince pupils that he was more than about three years older than they were, he had grown a beard. No ordinary beard, it was more an intermittent collection of wiry brown hairs, instantly attracting to (then Mr) McKechnie the nickname 'Pubechin'. He suffered in silence for at least two years but his decision to shave the beard for Charity Week merely reduced him to the nickname 'Pubeless' so the beard was quickly readopted. Dr McKechnie took all this in characteristic good humour, writing a column for *The Pelican* under the pseudonym 'Barbillus'. His good nature was endless, allowing the standard 'two sides' punishment to include pictures even when Anthony Scott crawled behind him to measure the width of his flares.

The Perse in the 1980s was much as any ex-Direct Grant school must have been: filled with bright pupils, eccentric teachers, and trying to find its feet for the expansion and change that stemmed from the move to fully Independent status. Otherwise, school life was much as it must have been in the 1970s and in the 1990s. Long summer afternoons after exams were over, sitting watching the 1st XI whilst listening to '99 Red Balloons' on our Walkmans. A first taste of true

*[In fact a tally of Rugby, Hockey and Cricket results show that First team honours were slightly in favour of the Perse, with several boys winning International Caps for Hockey.    Ed.]*

*Dr McKechnie, minus Robin Reliant, waiting to board the coach on a Third Form field trip in October 1985*

freedom away from parental (or seemingly any) control on the excellent school skiing trips. Listening to Tom Findlay and Jimmy Greenwood playing *Dr Beat* on the Record player in the Junior Mummery during Arts Week (it seems to have made a lasting impression on Tom). The relentless school sense of humour, with a kissogram confronting Mr Melville on-stage at assembly; the traditional Sixth Form pranks on its own final day (such as tying a giant, inflatable banana to the spire, or the prefects all arriving at assembly in drag); and the possibly-mythical tale of boys crawling through the loft in the administration wing, removing a ceiling tile and looking down on Mr Melville administering the cane to one of their friends.

The 1980s were a happy time, perhaps surprisingly free of growing pains, for a quirky but increasingly large and self-confident school.

## THE PERSE IN THE 1990s

*By JAMES WATSON, Senior Prefect 2000-2001*

The most noticeable development to have taken place during my time at the Perse has been the expansion of the School. When I joined, there was plenty of room for the approximately 460 boys to sit in the assembly hall, whereas now, the nearly 600 students often find it rather a tight fit! No wonder the Head of the School now dismisses the students at the end of the Assembly based on where they sit rather than by listing each form in turn. In September 1994, it took Iain Lunt only a few minutes to dismiss nineteen forms by name, but if Peter Caffall tried to dismiss thirty forms in 2001, the last to be dismissed would probably be better missing the rest of period one and moving straight to period two! This increase in the number of forms is slightly deceptive; the class sizes are now smaller (thankfully) than the thirty people of whom I was one during my first two years.

*David Roulinson looks down from the Mummery in 1999*

More students inevitably mean more teachers, and there have certainly been many new faces over the past decade. Five new teachers (or "masters" as I soon realised I was to call them!) joined with my year in 1994 (including our Headmaster, Mr Richardson), whereas in more recent years the number has sometimes been nearly double that. It has been strange when teachers who have joined during my time at the Perse have left before me, and this is not a rare phenomenon, but stranger still was the feeling when many of the long-serving masters (some of more than thirty years service) retired.

Rather like the "Millennium Bug", the transition to the two-week timetable was greatly anticipated but fortunately failed to wreak havoc on the School in September 2000. That was the second big timetabling change since I joined, the first having been the abolition of Saturday morning school at the end of my first year. I still remember the joy on other boys' faces as Mr Richardson announced the decision, as when it was announced that girls would be joining the Sixth Form, but I also remember a slightly downcast Sixth Form who had missed out on both counts! September 1995 was thus one of the most significant and initially strange beginnings of years I can remember. Whilst some lament the passing of Saturday morning school (and a few the infamous S.A.D. – Saturday Afternoon Detention) they are in a great minority, whereas everyone acknowledges that if the girls were now to leave, the School would certainly miss them.

*At Delphi on the Classics trip to Greece, April 2000. James Watson is second from the left*

Whilst I remember my own First Form days fondly, since I have been privileged to be One Alpha's Form Prefect during my final year here, I can see how many changes have been effected to the benefit of all. My First Form had one tutor for all thirty boys; now they have two tutors, each dealing with about twelve each. The same principle works in the Middle School too, and means that boys inevitably can receive greater attention. They might not realise or want this, but ultimately, they should be glad of it. The appointment of Heads of Lower and Middle School (and subsequently their deputies!) has occurred during my time, and no one can doubt the immense contribution that they have made to the School.

It is impossible to generalise about changes in teaching methods over the past decade, for each member of staff will work differently. Related to this, however, is the departure of the Mummery method of teaching English, particularly to Lower School boys, that occurred with David Roulinson's retirement in 1999. Proof of the fact that this was a well-known aspect of the School was given to me by a visitor at a subsequent Open Day who wanted to be shown the Mummery. Whatever one thinks about the "Play Way" and its replacement, no one can deny that an interesting feature of the School disappeared in the last decade, and I hope that successive generations at least know of it as a part of their School's history.

*Perse boys in Morocco, 2001*

Few people are actually concerned about the School history, but I admit that I have enjoyed finding out about it. The diversity that the School nurtures, however, meant that as I was looking at archives, there was probably someone playing roller-hockey, someone else feeding gerbils, another student juggling and yet another singing in the choir. The number of opportunities offered by the School, considerable already when I joined, has increased further and further. I refer here to the extra-curricular activities, and everyone owes a debt to the School in this respect. Whatever a student's interest, there is a society to develop it (or else one can be established!); the chances that dramatists, musicians, sportsmen and sportswomen have to improve and demonstrate their prowess are there for the taking. Beyond that, the many different trips the School organises are also much appreciated and often useful as well as enjoyable. I have been to Greece, Italy, Russia, France and Belgium with the School, but to demonstrate the variety, sports teams have been to Australia, Barbados and South Africa, the Venture Scouts have been to Africa and Iceland, Business students have been to Disneyland and Spain, Geographers have visited Morocco and linguists and musicians have been to Germany. Such a choice seems bewildering, but anyone who has been on any of these trips, or other ones within the British Isles, will acknowledge the benefit of such a visit. Thus the School's extra curricular activities, including CCF and Community Service, have continued to develop and are beneficial and complement the academic work of the School.

I have yet to mention the most significant part of the School collectively: the pupils.

Without them, there would be no Perse, and so a reader may be wondering whether they have changed at all during my time here. In many respects, they have not. There are still some unpleasant characters who see fit to upset their fellow-pupils or annoy teachers and so forth, but not noticeably more than when I joined in 1994 – a significant minority. The School is very good at dealing with such problems, as I can vouch from personal experience, after a problem I was having was resolved within a few hours. The largely problem-free atmosphere of the Perse has been achieved in a School which feels perceptibly less strict than 1994. Prefects, for instance, are now advised not to dole out eight sides on the subject of the inside of a ping-pong ball simply because a first former is moderately annoying, even if more recent prefects have been heard by me exclaiming "we get no respect".

Respect, though, has to be earned, and that inevitably means hard work. the Perse remains a School where industry is crucial, both in academic terms and beyond the curriculum too. This is just how it should be, and if some say "take the easy life" and do not involve themselves in the life of the School, then they are missing out. I owe the Perse a great deal, both in terms of my development as a person and the opportunities it has given me.

My time at the Perse then has seen many changes, but beneath them all, the School remains, as it always should, in my opinion, a place where diversity, friendliness and industry are encouraged and rewarded.

*Qui facit per alium facit per se*

## *Afterword*

*by NIGEL RICHARDSON (Headmaster since 1994)*

Those of us who joined the Perse long after the momentous events which form the central theme of this publication see them through the eyes of an outsider. I have walked round the perimeter of the buildings many times, and found myself thinking as I go: "Those who achieved the move from Gonville Place to Hills Road, were men of remarkable vision. Stubbs had been Headmaster of the Perse for fifteen years by 1960, with less than a decade to retirement. Even allowing for the length of time that a move had been in the air, it would surely have been easier for him to have settled for a quieter and more predictable life." At that point I usually find myself thinking how fortunate we are that they were prepared to make the effort.

Those of us who came later owe them a huge debt. There are inevitable economies of scale in good schools these days which have prompted our steady growth from just over 400 pupils to our present 600. Without this growth, we would have been much more strategically boxed in. And without the move to Hills Road, the Perse today would be on a totally constricted site, hemmed in not just by other buildings, but also by ceaseless traffic noise, a total lack of parking, and above all very little space in which to develop.

Increasing numbers of cars would have made journeys to the games fields extremely slow; we are immensely fortunate in having most of our games facilities on site. Moreover, many of the changes in schools over the past forty years which the School has already been able to reflect would have been far more difficult to achieve - the growth of drama and music, the move within teaching areas towards coursework storage, increasingly specialized laboratory and teaching equipment, back-up via Information Technology, television and video. The spectacular physical size of the modern British teenager compared with pupils of earlier generations would have made life in the old buildings far from easy.

Where does our physical development go from here? Schools like the Perse strive to provide a varied and ambitious extra-curricular programme, as well as remaining high up in national academic league tables. These aims, together with the need to attract high-calibre staff at a time when the national pool of those available is shrinking, all suggest that the continuing development of specialist buildings needs to go on (alongside the building - up of a bursary endowment fund to keep pupil access broad). Schools will go on attracting top-class staff – and pupils – in the furure only if they can give them the plant they deserve in which to practise their skills. As more funds are allocated to the maintained sector, independent schools will need to show that they offer significantly more, to a parent clientele which will become even more discriminating about value for money.

We are now a 3–18 series of schools for many Pelican/Perse families, even though transfer between schools is subject to academic criteria, and we still open only to boys in the years between 7 and 16. We aim to build a new Hall at the Pelican pre-prep (formerly Northwold House) and an Arts Centre at the Prep when funds allow. Our immediate aim at the Prep is to extend Science and Information Technology facilities by September 2002.

On the Hills Road site, the footprint for future development of the Upper School has become much clearer with the decision to move the Sixth Form Centre to the northern end of the Sports Centre in September 2000. We hope to extend the Music School (the one remaining project from the 1997 Millennium Campaign not yet tackled), in 2000-2003. Thereafter we have plans to extend the library (now in the former Sixth Form Centre) both across the courtyard towards its former home and into the area next to the Common Room. We would like to extend both the Common Room itself (in recognition of the fact that we now have nearly 50% more teachers than we had at the time when it was built), and the Technology part of the CCF building adjacent to the Parade Ground.

I have a feeling that anyone returning to the site for the fiftieth anniversary of the move will also need to take a close look at two other areas. Firstly, the space between the present administration building (just to the right of the main entrance) and the Macfarlane-Grieve pavilion. It would be a great pity totally to block the view across to the First XI square; on the other hand there is scope for a really imaginative building which preserves the vista. Secondly we have a key strategic space in the form of the old gymnasium – which needs a mezzanine floor. This might incorporate an extended gallery to the Hall and something like a studio theatre at first floor level. We also need more catering facilties down below; the travel patterns in and around Cambridge suggest that our future lies in providing breakfast and maybe tea or supper for those who cannot easily get into or out of the City at peak travel times.

And yet... it is easy to get carried away about what we would ideally like to have in the years to come. A look at the photographs of the "new" School in 1960 gives a timely reminder of how carefully the funds available for the project were spent, and few of the *present* buildings were in existence in the early years after the move. At their heart is a main building which has stood the test of time remarkably well. It was also highly adventurous in its time – just before New Cambridge architecture changed the face of many parts of the local landscape to the north of us.

Stanley Stubbs and his generation were people of great foresight - and they were thrifty, making good use of what they had. It is surely right that we should commemorate their vision in this fortieth anniversary publication which David Jones has compiled with such skill.

## BIBLIOGRAPHY

1. **School archive records**
   *The Pelican*
   *The Old Persean Chronicle*
   Perse Governors' Minute Book (1950s)
   Appeal brochures for 1958, 1979, 1988, 1997
   Programme for the Opening Ceremony, 3rd July 1961
   HMI Inspection Reports 1930 (interim), 1935, 1951
   Mitchell, S.J.D. *John Barrow Allen: A Victorian Headmaster* (*The Pelican*, Summer 1975)
   Newscuttings File *The Times*, The *Cambridge Daily News*, The *Cambridge Evening News*

2. **The Cambridgeshire Collection, Lion Yard**
   Newscuttings   Perse File
   Ordnance Survey Maps, Cambridge   6ins to 1 mile 1904 & 1927  (sheet 47 NW & SW)

3. **Books**
   *Dictionary of National Biography*
   Gardner, B. *The Public Schools* (Hamish Hamilton 1973)
   Gray, J.M. *A History of the Perse School, 1615-1976*  (Bowes & Bowes 1921)
   Henderson, R.J. *A History of King's College Choir School* (King's College Choir School 1981)
   HMSO *Royal Commission on Historical Monuments: The City of Cambridge*, Volume 1
      (HMSO 1959)
   Holford, W. & Myles Wright, H. *Cambridge Planning Proposals* (CUP 1950)
   Mitchell, S.J.D. *Perse: A History of the Perse School, 1615-1976* (Oleander 1976)
   Percival, A.C. *The Origins of the Headmasters' Conference* (John Murray 1969)
   Pevsner, N. *The Buildings of England: Cambridgeshire* (Penguin 1970, Second Edition)
   Reé, H. *Educator Extraordinary: the Life and Achievement of Henry Morris 1888-1961*
   (Peter Owen 1985)
   Rodgers, J. *The Old Public Schools of England* (Batsford 1938)
   Seaborne, M. *The English School, its Architecture and Organisation 1370-1870*
      (RKP 1971)
   Seaborne, M. *The Architecture of the Victorian Public School; essay in The Victorian
      Public School*, ed. Simon, B. and Bradley, I (Gill and Macmillan 1975)
   Stray, C. *The Living Word: W.H.D. Rouse and the Crisis Of Classics in Edwardian
      England* (Bristol Classical Press 1992)
   Stubbings, F.H. *Forty-nine Lives* (Emmanuel College 1983)
   Taylor, N. *Cambridge New Architecture* (Trinity Hall 1964)
   Willis & Clark *The Architectural History of the University of Cambridge* Vols III and IV
      (CUP 1886)

4. **Miscellaneous**
   Anon 'The New Look of a 350-year-old School'; in *East Anglian Life* August 1964
   Benson, A.C. Manuscript diaries Vols 145 p11-12 and 149 p39 (Magdalene College)
   Parry, C. 'A Specialist Room for English'; in *School and College* January 1965
   University of Cambridge Local Examinations Syndicate, pamphlet on the new
      Syndicate buildings (10 pages) 29th April 1965
   R.E.W. 'Perse School Cambridge'; in *London John* March 1961 p7 (one page article in
      the magazine of construction firm John Mowlem & Co. Ltd.).